Liberating Ourselves

Liberating Ourselves

Attaining Personal Freedom to Release Creative Potential

Scott Teitsworth

© 2016 Scott Teitsworth

All Rights Reserved.

ISBN-10: ISBN-10: 0-9971416-0-3
ISBN-13: 978-0-9971416-0-3

Published by
Wetware Media, LLC
www.wetwaremedia.com

This publication is intended to provide accurate and authoritative information in regard to the subject matter covered. It is sold with the understanding that the publisher is not engaged in rendering psychological, financial, legal, or other professional services. If expert assistance or counseling is needed, the services of a competent professional should be sought.

Contents

Preface...9

1. Is There Any Point to Spirituality? 11

2. Can Science and Spirituality Coexist? 30

3. Freeing a Whale Caught in Nets 46

4. How Yoga Helps Us Break Free...............65

5. The Role of The Chakras....................81

6. Healing the Ego 99

7. Concluding Thoughts.....................112

About the Author..........................117

For More Information......................119

Preface

Why do we bother to search? What is it that brings us to determine that our comfortable, more or less pleasant life is not adequate and that we need to look for something more?

We can stay distracted from this discomfort for a long time, but it doesn't rid us of that lingering, nagging doubt about our lives. Digging deeper is the real cure. But how do we dig deeper?

This small book is a treasure trove of practical wisdom. It is the result of several interviews with author and teacher of Indian philosophy, Scott Teitsworth. (The collected audio recordings of these interviews is available at all major on line audio book retailers, published under the same title: *Liberating Ourselves*.)

In these interviews, Teitsworth shares examples of digging deeper—the profound insights of Indian psychology and philosophy in language readily accessible to the modern seeker of truth. He emphasizes how to apply this ancient wisdom in a practical manner so that we might optimize our personal freedom, minimize the effects of stress and trauma, and release untapped creative abilities.

It takes courage to relax our defense system and dig deeper. But if we don't, we are doomed to a mediocre life and a life of

LIBERATING OURSELVES

conflict. But Scott's message is encouraging and inspiring: "Know that freedom is possible. Choose it, allow it, enjoy it—and laugh a little!"

1

Is There Any Point to Spirituality?

The Yoga of Liberation

I have been very fortunate to be associated with one of the major characters of the human race—a man named Narayana Guru who is strangely unknown outside of the southern tip of India. He lived from around 1850 to 1928, and he inspired what may be the largest peaceful revolution that we know of. He transformed a very decadent, feudal society with severe caste distinctions into modern Kerala—the poster child for a healthy society and a shining example of what's possible for humanity. And yet, in the West, Narayana Guru remains largely unappreciated.

Although Narayana Guru is thought of as a social reformer, he was primarily a philosopher and mystic. His social reforms grew out of his mystical vision of the unity of all life. His primary disciple was Nataraja Guru, who realized that the world was changing, and that in order to expand his guru's vision, he needed to include Western science. Narayana Guru understood this and sent Nataraja Guru to the Sorbonne for a doctorate. In Nataraja, the Western perspective of rationality and science merged perfectly with Narayana Guru's mystical vision. I do not know of any person in whom there is such a fine blending of science and mysticism.

Nataraja Guru's audience was mid 20th century intellectuals, so his books are difficult for the average Western reader to understand. Fortunately, he had a disciple, Nitya Chaitanya Yati, who was bright enough to understand the complicated philosophy and science and was also able to present it in terms accessible to the average Westerner. He was able to translate it in such a way that made it very exciting and transformative for those of us who are not geniuses or well-versed in philosophy.

Nitya was my guru and I worked very closely with him to make this unique philosophy a part of my life, and I want to present an overview of it in this book. It is an exceptionally practical philosophy. It points directly to our lives, teaching us how to energize our own potentials.

Many practical philosophies are about learning what somebody else has discovered and then trying to imitate that. This philosophy is about learning to be authentically ourselves, without imitation. It's incredibly exciting every time you regain some of your own territory. It's a leap of great improvement in your life. And it is permanent. It is an understanding that can't be taken away from you. A lot of spiritual practices are built up piece by piece. You're supposed to learn this, and then you learn that, and then you learn the next thing—all to achieve some high aim. But this is really about Understanding—Understanding with a capital U.

IS THERE ANY POINT TO SPIRITUALITY?

There are a lot of wonderful stories about Narayana Guru. He was once visited by Mahatma Gandhi and is credited with changing Gandhi's attitude about the caste system in India. Gandhi was originally a proponent of caste, but Narayana Guru was able to convince him that it was not in anyone's interest. Because of this, Gandhi came to see that caste was a stumbling block to the progress of India. Gandhi's revolution, even though it was based in passivism, produced a lot of bloodshed. Amazingly, in Narayana Guru's revolution there were some tensions, but I don't believe there were any deaths. It was a totally peaceful revolution that inspired people to just start living correctly. He believed that we're all one family and that the downtrodden are equal to the rich and powerful. He believed that girls were equal to boys and should be sent to school. But he never let his followers introduce these ideals into society with any kind of aggression. He insisted on peaceful means.

Once he was giving a speech to a huge crowd, and there was a stirring agitation in the back of the auditorium. He asked "What's going on?" The people said, "There's this 'untouchable' boy trying to come to the meeting." They were trying to push this so-called untouchable boy out. Narayana Guru just brought the boy up to the stage to sit with him. He didn't say anything, but simply put him in a chair next to him. After a while the Guru went on with his speech. And the entire crowd was transformed by that act. The boy eventually became part of Narayana Guru's entourage.

LIBERATING OURSELVES

It's unfortunate that the scientific community has been put off by the wishful thinking and silly projections of some spiritual programs and faith-based ideologies. The philosophy that we're exploring here doesn't require any of that. This is a philosophy that science can embrace.

In these pages I will share some examples of transformative ideas and insights into how we can have our own personal and peaceful revolution. When we have a peaceful revolution in own lives, it impacts everything around us and helps to bring about the peaceful revolution that we very desperately need on this planet. This process is the Yoga of Liberation.

The Search

Perhaps the first question is why do we bother to search? What is it that brings us to determine that our comfortable, more or less pleasant life is not adequate and that we need to look for something better?

Our life starts very much like the universe. First there's a big bang and then there's a period of hyperinflation, followed by steady growth, and even accelerating growth, like the universe is having right now.

Everybody is pretty clear on the fact that in utero, there's a guiding force that allows for miraculous orderly development of all the parts, resulting, in most cases, in a perfect outcome. We mistakenly believe this miraculous orderly development ends at the moment of birth and that from then on we're on our own. But it doesn't stop at birth. It continues. Using little bonnets of electrodes, scientists have observed babies to determine what they're thinking. They see that there's a "passing of the torch," so to speak, from this inner guide that's been controlling their development in the womb to the babies' cortex. They see a back-and-forth, a wrestling or teaching process going on, until eventually the cortex assumes command.

The Inner Guide

My interpretation of this process is that the cortex has promised never to forget its inner guide. It seems so natural! Yet after birth, while this guide is not actually gone, it is forgotten and overlaid by all of the distractions, demands and pressures of outward life. Despite this, throughout our lives, even as we get farther and farther away from it consciously, there's part of us that remembers we're missing something important in our life. Sometimes we're given prescription medications to forget the pain of separation. Or we self-medicate. Or we're distracted by our cool gizmos or by the pressures of trying to fit into society as we imagine it's supposed to work. Many factors work to lead us away from recognizing our inner guidance system.

Should we reconnect with this inner guide? Why?

LIBERATING OURSELVES

The people who exhibit genius in creativity are the people who have maintained contact with this inner guide. The inner guidance system represents 99.9% of our capacity. The cortex is a very small part of our entire brain. The neuroscientist David Eagleman compares it to a stowaway on an ocean liner. We think we're piloting the ship, but in fact we are in the cargo hold getting a ride. The ship is going places about which we have no idea, but we're down there imagining that we're somehow in control.

Observation through functional MRI shows that the brain goes through significant thinking and processing to come to the point where the person says "I just thought of something." Neuroscientists have decided that we don't actually have free will because all of this stuff is going on behind the scenes. We think we've thought of something, but it's already well prepared for us.

One of the jokes of modern science is that religion has historically been blamed for man's lack of free will and his bondage, and science has been praised for espousing free will and independence. But now religion may be the last vestige of free will because modern science is saying we don't have any. It tells us that we're bound and fully condemned to do what our genes and conditioning forces us to do.

I think this current science is wrong. I think that we have much more potential than that. If we think of ourselves as the entire ocean liner and not just the small ego stowed way in the cargo hold, then free will can operate in the very the intelligent, deep levels of ourselves. The cortex's role is to give its motivations its blessing. I think eventually we will have the scientific basis for understanding this connection between the cortex and the rest of ourselves, and we will all be much happier, more creative and interesting people.

So here's what winds up happening: We are born, and at first we're disappointed. There's a period of real resentment in young childhood when, after having a had great time running all over the ship in utero, we are forced, in early life, to accept our little room in the cargo hold of this ocean liner. Then we start school and have to begin to face so called "reality." The room in the cargo hold gets even smaller. And basically what we do for the rest of our life is redecorate our little room to try to make it more attractive to visitors, to impress people, and hopefully to get our meal ticket. A very great deal of what we do is just moving the furniture around in this little room. No one is being encouraged to step outside, because it's a bit scary. If you peek out the door, it's dark and vast and unknown. Unless we have someone who is helping us or directing us to peek outside, we're very likely to say, "This is it. This is all I am. This is safe. There are no monsters here as far as I can tell, so I'll just stay right here."

Psychedelics

When psychedelics are used as part of a growth training process, it allows for a brief glimpse of the whole ship. We're reminded that we're much more than we think we are. That "more" is something we can definitely explore and reconnect with.

LIBERATING OURSELVES

Science is finally catching up to ancient wisdom and ratifying it—though scientists do not even know that they're ratifying it, because they don't know the ancient wisdom. I happen to have studied the ancient wisdom, so I really enjoy the fact that it is finding its way to into scientific understanding.

One of the many exciting areas of scientific exploration is observing people taking the psychedelic drug psilocybin under functional MRI. Prior to these recent experiments, the expectation was that the brain was going to wildly light up with activity as a result of all the hallucinations and insights that people experience while taking psilocybin. Obviously the brain is very active. So with great anticipation, the researchers put a bunch of poor tripping guys into the MRI.

Researchers discovered the opposite of what they expected to find. There is very little visible activity. The cortex basically shuts down and the rest of the brain is not particularly visible in the MRI. Obviously what is being experienced by psychedelic adventurers is beyond the ego/cortex. Essentially, the cortex is put to sleep for a while and everything else that we are comes out.

The feeling I often had when taking psychedelics was, "Oh my God, here I am again. I'm home. This is me!" The "me" is the rest of the ocean liner and the "home again" sensation was the experience of reacquainting myself with it. It's a transformative experience. Jokingly I say that a guided psychedelic experience should be an elective in high school all over the world. But in fact, the more I look into the ancient cultures, including Greece and

India, that used psychedelics as a rite of passage, the more I see that they all had periods of great blossoming as a result of its use. There are certainly other ways to have such insights. Near-death experiences and shocks to the nervous system force us "out of the cargo hold". Conflict also often prompts us to remember that our current room is not adequate. We must learn to recognize these moments as clearly as we recognize the transformative value of a supervised psychedelic event.

Digging In

We are vast beings crammed into a small space by our many constraints, and it's not comfortable. It's not okay. One of the clues that it is not okay is that we become bored or unhappy. These feelings should be telling us to do something different, to dig deeper or look around. But social pressure says instead we should get drunk, or take some antidepressants, or look at a cool new app. We can stay distracted for a long time, but it doesn't get rid us of that lingering, nagging doubt about our lives. Digging deeper is the real cure. But do we choose to dig deeper? That is the question. What the *Bhagavad Gita* says is that only one in a thousand seeks a way out of their cramped quarters, and of those, only one in a thousand actually succeeds in getting out. We're talking about almost vanishingly small numbers.

So this "digging deeper" is a rare thing. And yet we live in a time when there's been an explosion of people exploring and digging deeper. There are a lot of available self-exploration techniques out there if we decide to open ourselves up to them. Unfortunately, a lot of them are not very good and there are many stories of tragedies and indignities. So it's not just that we should stroll out and take whatever comes along. We have to maintain a cautious, skeptical attitude through all of our searching. This skepticism is something that a lot of spiritual teachers ask us to surrender because they equate it with clinging to our little room in the cargo hold of the ocean liner. So we have to be smart. We must be open to what they tell us, and we must move on if it doesn't feel right.

Simultaneously, we have to be aware of our resistance. We really have to be full participants in this process. The ego is very clever and quick to co-opt almost everything. It will decorate that little room with spiritual posters and inspiring paintings and so many lovely things until our room is so beautiful that we think this must be liberation. It feels pretty good. This is where having help is really important. Help from someone else who can see that you actually haven't gone as far as you think you have, and can make some practical suggestions.

Losing Our Inner Authority

I want to mention one of the problems we often encounter: As small children, we are forced to cede our inner authority to other people. We're directed by adults who are certain that they know better than we do. In fact, they're just slightly older versions of us who have been through the same hell of giving up all of their integrity to society. They really don't know more than we do; they're just pretending to. But we go ahead and buy into it. We say, "Okay, they're the authorities." The "authorities" include our parents and teachers, religious dogma, the police, and the government. We need to reclaim our inner authority lest we fall victim to charlatans and swindlers who say, "Oh, I'm in charge here. Look how wonderful and rich and beautiful I am. I know all of the Scripture. Or all of Business. Come on, I'll show you the way." Beware of this dangerous lure. And rest assured that people who really know what they're talking about don't send out lures like that.

I still remember driving to the beach after training with my teacher about inner authenticity and suddenly realizing that I had been bowing down to various authorities for my whole life—and that these authorities were just as in the dark as I was (or more so). With that insight, a huge boulder was lifted off my psyche. I actually burst out laughing! It was such a relief to realize that all of these authority figures were just false fronts for people who were as confused and in doubt as I was. They were just pretending. It was a good shtick for them, a con job. This realization changed my life. From that moment on, I've had successful interactions with all sorts of authority figures because I don't treat them as authority figures. I just treat them as fellow human beings who are in the same pickle I'm in. I don't bow down and cringe before them or act like a willing servant. They are just regular people. And so am I. It's amazing that a moment's insight like that can have such a profound effect on a life—my life, your life, our lives.

LIBERATING OURSELVES

We also buy into the theory that spiritual transformation is more or less like a nuclear explosion…that it's this huge blast that strips away everything we are and replaces it with something else. We think of it as a vast, momentary, spectacular event. It makes for really good stories. Spiritual literature is full of them. But in fact, for the most part, spiritual transformation is nothing like that. Small incremental wisdoms can change our lives profoundly once we really make our lives our own.

Here's an example that is specific to me, but probably common to everyone. As a child, I loved classical music and playing the piano. When I become a teenager, I was shown the potential of yoga through LSD experiences. I should mention that when I had a really fantastic breakthrough trip on LSD, where I realized that I had experienced the state that all seers talk about. "This is the place that we should find ourselves in. This is who we really are," I thought to myself. I realized that the yoga teachers of history were giving techniques in order to access that place. And I thought, "Okay, this is what I want to do. I want to spend my life doing yoga and regaining this state because it's so fantastic. And that means I should give up everything, including playing music. I'll get a job to support myself and I'll just do yoga." Very quickly I met a good teacher. I was very fortunate because I might have easily been led astray by a charlatan in my eager state. My teacher was a tough minded, scientifically grounded man from southern India who agreed to take me on and teach me. We lived together in a house in Portland, Oregon. People came to our classes and often invited us out to dinner. One night he and I went to a place that had a piano and I played on it after dinner. When we were driving home, my teacher said, "You know, yoga doesn't have to be sitting in lotus pose with your eyes rolled up. Yoga can be anything you do, whatever you do, whatever you *love* to do. Music is a fine form of yoga." And from that very moment, I started playing the piano again.

I realized that he was correct. Music is a fantastic yoga program, because as soon as you have a distraction you make mistakes, so it teaches you to concentrate and focus. And it sounds beautiful! It resonated with what I loved. Resonating with what one loves is really how we know that we're on the right track and we're tuned into our *dharma*. Soon enough I was playing up to 16 or 18 hours a day. I got the Beethoven sonatas and I couldn't believe how wonderful they were. I read through them endlessly, getting better and better. I was so excited! Then I started to sense that something wasn't quite right. And as I was doing my musical meditation, I paid attention to this nagging doubt until I eventually detected what it was. As a kid, I played fairly well and my family had always gathered around the piano to praise me. They were very excited about my talent. They admired me. I realized that part of me had never let go of that pleasure. I was still playing in hopes of being admired and loved and appreciated, and I realized that was an impediment to my being fully involved with music. Recognizing this was an important step in my evolution as a mature artist. It prompted me to take back the inner musical authority that, as a child, I had ceded to my family and admirers. I became free to really play the music.

The reason I say this kind of experience is universal is that, although you probably didn't play the piano, you did something as a child to make people love you. You may have done any number of things. The natural inclinations that won you love as a child and the rewards you got from them may have been subtle, but they were there. Unfortunately, as you matured, they became extra baggage—ego baggage really—that kept you from really "owning" your inclinations. We need to throw off this old conditioning in order to be free.

This business of trying to be free of the "performance for praise" constellation was not easy work. It took me quite a bit of time. Every time it came up, I'd acknowledge it: "Oh, there it is again. There's that little part of me that wants people to love me for playing the piano for them." For a while I over compensated by reacting negatively to people's praise for my playing because it reactivated the old feelings. But eventually I did get free of them. I came to a neutral place. That's real yoga.

The Essence of Yoga

The essence of yoga is trying to come to a balance between two sides of two poles or the "two horns of a dilemma." All of the problems that we face in life come as dual problems—of good and bad, right and wrong, up and down, and so on. If we stick to one side or the other, then we lose our balance. Yoga is the process of using our intelligence to envision the entire situation and find the neutral balance point in the middle of it. It brings very freeing, liberating insights. The result is freedom.

One of the primary questions that you must ask when you're looking for someone to work with is "How much do I allow myself to be drawn out of my comfort zone?" And in this regard, I think that viewing the entire universe as our guru or therapist is essential. Don't locate this principle in a single individual. It's too much pressure on them. If you're lucky—and again this is vanishingly rare—but if you're lucky enough to find a great personal teacher or guru and you feel trust and safeness in their presence, then that's fine. But most of us will never have that. We may think we don't have access to a guru because we don't have access to someone special like that. But, in fact, the universe is very available and very kind. It wants to teach us in all sorts of ways, and when we get stuck, it will throw waves against our shores to try to break up our blocks. All we really need to do is be open to life as it comes to us. Actually, I shouldn't say that's all we need to do because we often don't even realize how blocked we are to being open. But if we start to tell ourselves that the universe contains a teaching principle, an enlightening principle, it will help us to evolve.

Look around. Everything has evolved, and that itself is a miracle. In fact, I have an old article from *Scientific American*, where one of the scientists finally uses the "G" word. He mentions God. He says that all of this evolution, all of these leaps of emergent phenomena, are just what God is. We don't call it that anymore. It's an old-fashioned term. But that's exactly what it is. The universe seems to be predisposed to making these huge leaps of evolution. And not just on the macrocosmic scale, but on the personal scale, too. If we open ourselves to what's around us, we see what the universe is trying to teach us. We must always keep our common sense, however. If things are suggested that are dangerous and foolhardy, don't do them.

"I am the Absolute"

We all somehow believe that we have to be someone other than ourselves in order to be okay. But in the Indian teaching of Vedanta, the theory is that we are actually perfectly okay to start with, and as soon as we get all the junk that we accumulate through life out of the way, we restore ourselves to that perfectly okay state. Basically, one of the mantras to think about is "That Thou Art," *tat tvam asi,* or "The Absolute is what I am." We are perfection itself, and we are part of that evolutionary process. We've developed a number of blocks however, so this type of spirituality is a path of removing the impediments to being ourselves. If we can do that, we become creative geniuses.

Buckminster Fuller is a perfect example of this. He considered himself, and I believe he was, a failure after college. He attributed his failure to all the pat answers and dried up beliefs that had been instilled in him during his training. He realized he was trying to please other people, and in doing so he had given up himself completely. He hadn't done well in school and his businesses didn't work out, but he did an amazing thing. He took two years off and went into silence, and in that period of silence and intense self-examination, he questioned everything. He questioned every idea that came up. In these two years, he basically didn't say a word. He just concentrated. And when he was finished, he had restored himself to himself. Now he's legendary as one of the great creative thinkers of the twentieth century.

My teacher did the same thing. Nitya spent almost two years in isolation, after he freaked out with his guru and decided that everybody was nuts and everything was all wrong. He went into a little cabin for eighteen months, and it changed his life. He has written some wonderful pieces about the transformation he underwent in that situation. It's pretty neat to find out that Bucky did the same thing. If you don't know about Bucky Fuller, it's fun to read about him because he was so iconoclastic, funny, and brilliant. He came up with many useful inventions that we still employ. He embodied the kind of transformation back to ourselves that I'm talking about here.

I was recently at a convention, a kind of "Lake Wobegon" gathering, where everybody was "above average." It was a group of highly intelligent people. For some reason, I wound up being with the teenagers. They were really interesting, very bright, kids. We talked about success and the road to success. All of them had this vision of, "Okay, I'm going to graduate from high school, I'm going to go to the college of my choice, and here are the programs I'm going to follow…Then when I graduate, I'm going to do postgraduate work in this field, and then I will be able to do what I want, which is this…" They had all planned out very long programs with distant rewards. What I didn't say, but what I knew, was that after you finish all that schooling and start working, there's a whole new set of things that you discover you're supposed to work for. You work for those things, and then you work for your retirement, and then, when you retire, you work for, I don't know, a better burial plot or something. It's a program, a game, that can keep you looking to the future and dissatisfied with your current position at all times. My contribution to those kids was to say, "Please, think of yourselves as successes right now. You guys are miracles. You are so wonderful in so many ways and you're thinking that you have to become this scientist in this lab or that technical wizard in a garage somewhere in 20 years. That's who you think you are, but you're who you are now!" I hope it sank in.

This "future game" has created a malaise that permeates our culture. No one dares to think of themselves as okay. And the feedback we often get is that we're not okay. Parents show us what we're supposed to be. Schools teach us what we're supposed to be. Kids tease us for being ourselves, so we think, "Gosh, I don't want to be like that. I don't dare express myself." All of these things become the burden that we bear because we're too timid to do what Buckminster Fuller or other brave souls have done, and that is: throw it all off! Break it up into pieces, smash it, pulverize it, mix it with water and turn it into mud and wash it away. Get those wrong ideas, get that burden, out of our system.

IS THERE ANY POINT TO SPIRITUALITY?

When I tell my Western students that Vedantins meditate on being the Absolute and that that's the key to everything, they're horrified. In our culture, we assume God is far away and we are these miserable sinners groveling about and hoping for grace and some kind of a break. This attitude, which exists even in atheists, is widespread. The notion that "I" can be anything like the Absolute is extremely radical to Westerners. I am amazed at the negative reactions that this thought brings up. It shows just how radically we have become separated from our true nature.

The question often came up, "If you thing you're God or the Absolute, does that mean your ego is going to be as big as the whole sky?" Well, it could of course. But that's not the way this meditation was intended. The idea of perfection is a worthy subject for meditation—much better than a remote God or any of that stuff. We should encourage young people to explore who they actually are in their unadulterated state and let that inform their thinking about what they want to be. We should stop supplying them with really boring, onerous tasks and then telling them to choose between packages A, B, C or D. Having a vision of what is possible and the desire to access it is an essential part of becoming an adult. That's perhaps why we have so few adults in our society.

Instead, let's realize we are perfect. We are so complicated and amazing. Every day we learn more about how amazing our psychophysical system is and yet we keep on thinking we've just got to get out of it and go somewhere else. No. We just have to use it, and get into it, and start to appreciate it. And then the sky's the limit.

Can Science and Spirituality Coexist?

Can science and spirituality ever agree on anything? Well, the simple answer is yes, of course. My teacher's teacher, Nataraja Guru, made it his main mission to develop a universal language that would unite all of the different factions of science and religion. My teachers always told me that there are not two truths. Truth is one thing. And spiritual people and scientists and even religious people are all trying to find that one truth. We all think the truth is important and we want to adhere to it. And we believe that it will make us happy and that it will make the world a better place. We all agree on these basic premises, so it's a good starting point.

Some of us think that religion is the cause of most the pain and misery of life, but, scientists are the ones who have invented atomic bombs and all sorts of weapons of war and different ways to commit genocide. Frankly, I don't think either side is squeaky clean. And that's another good starting place—the admission that neither the proponents of science nor of religion know everything. The impulse on anybody's part to convince everybody else that you know what you're talking about is very dangerous. It's something that we learn to do as children to protect ourselves when in fact we really don't know very much. Once you start admitting that you don't know, you allow the other person to have their faulty position too, and then you're not so likely to kill each other over it.

As I said in my introduction, Nataraja Guru spent a lot of time in Europe. He was sent by Narayana Guru, the founder of our lineage, to get his doctorate at the Sorbonne, where he was exposed to Western science and philosophy. One time in the mid 1950s, he was driving around with a disciple, and the car broke down right in front of the Royal Academy of Science in Brussels. The car repair was going to take a while, so he went inside. A conference was in progress. It was on the importance of trying to maintain contact between all of the different social and political groups in Europe.

This was post World War II, of course, so communication between factions was a very pressing issue. During the twentieth century, specialization had become extreme in all of the disciplines, and people in different areas of study realized they were losing contact with each other. So how could they stay in touch? Nataraja Guru fit right in to this conversation. He became a part of the convention and they even commissioned a paper on it from him. He spent the rest of his life basically trying to transmit a kind of general theory of consciousness using mathematical modeling and so on, that could be used as the basis of a universal language.

LIBERATING OURSELVES

Unfortunately, since the word guru (meaning simply remover of darkness) has negative connotations in the West, the name "Nataraja Guru" discouraged a lot of scientists from listening to him, so he never became as well known as he should have. But he did write a serious book called An Integrated Science of the Absolute and many other subsidiary writings that discuss how we can effectively communicate. Essentially communication requires leaving the diversity of separate points of view or disciplines and returning to a common ground from which all of those separate points of view evolved.

To demonstrate the value of this, here's a very poignant paragraph from Nataraja Guru's book, *Wisdom* (under the subtitle Unitive and Universal Approach Needed):

> There should no longer be cultural preserves or prerogatives which try to divide humanity into sheep or goats. The myth of the primitive or inferior man has to be abandoned. The orthodox and the heterodox, the conservative and the liberal, the rightist and the leftist, must be able to meet in the endeavor to preserve the best human heritage that belongs to all. A common cultural language, which would enable these precious values to be referred to, irrespective of the linguistic or traditional barriers, has to be evolved. Such a mathematically precise language would pave the way for the formulation of a regular science. Values preserved through humanistic studies could then be effectively cultivated without the arbitrary and sentimental barriers that history or

CAN SCIENCE AND SPIRITUALITY EXIST?

geography might interpose between people. An open, dynamic and positive scientific attitude must invade the closed, static and private preserves in which higher human values have hitherto remained enclosed. In other words, the challenge involved here is to bring back the humanities and the human values involved therein, into line with the other scientific values which, for no just reason, have in recent years tended to be considered as if divorced or disjunct from the former. (p. 183)

I'm pleased that this question about whether science and spirituality can coexist and agree on anything has come up. As I said earlier, this is a central impulse of my lineage. My teachers were excellent at maintaining a scientific perspective and bringing a wide variety of understanding into line with it. This is really the Indian tradition. The *Bhagavad Gita* says in numerous places that the highest form of sacrifice is the "wisdom sacrifice." It tells us that using our intelligence, our well-honed reason, to understand and connect with everything around us is the best way to seek truth. All other ways have their degrees of validity. Everything works to the degree that it's valid, but to seek to understand and connect with everything is the very best way of all.

When religious or scientific people ridicule each other, they often take the most absurd example as a straw man because it's easy to make fun of it or discredit it. The straw man is supposed to stand for the entire field. But in actuality, within both science and religion are many well-meaning and thoughtful people, caring people, compassionate people. We shouldn't get distracted by the absurdities and the loudmouths. There are scientific fundamentalists just like there are religious fundamentalists shaking their fists at each other and making fun of each other. But all that's really beside the point of a serious search for truth. It's a distraction. Instead, what we really have to do is to bring our understanding back to ourselves. Instead of feeling like we want to criticize everyone else, we have to look to our own faults. That becomes a very rich arena of work and one into which we are always granted entry if we knock on the door. The person who hates us is not going to listen to us and is not going to learn anything from us. But we can learn from ourselves, and we can learn a lot, if we are willing.

Science has recently caught up to the spiritual vision of the ancients in realizing that what looks like the world outside of us is actually a construct going on inside the brain. This is possibly the most shocking and disturbing realization anyone can have. We're so convinced that our sense input—what we see and hear and feel—is reality that we ignore the fact that it is actually an interpolation that our brain is making. Our brain is not unprejudiced. It is comparing the input of the senses with previous experience, which makes it smaller than it is. It shrinks it down, like Procrustes chopping up his visitors to make them fit into his little bed. It shrinks reality to fit our preconceptions.

Once we realize that this is what's going on, we can stop insisting that everyone fit our preconceptions and instead look at them as an opportunity to step outside of our preconceptions. I can accept that this person with whom I disagree is actually showing me something that I'm not allowing. Why is that? We should realize that inside the brain, everyone's brain, it is pitch black. The light that we think we see stops at the eye and does not go into the brain. It's dark in there. There's a little stage in there, a virtual stage, where the brain brilliantly models all of the static vibrations that are striking the body from all directions all the time, constantly making it coherent and meaningful according to what we believe. It is a miracle. And the most loathsome person—as well as the best person—is performing that miracle right in front of us. The fact that they can do that should make us feel loving and happy towards them instead of wanting to fight them. Of course we're going to see things differently, but isn't that wonderful!

Tracing back to the place where this urge to fight and do battle is seated is an important meditation and work for all people. But we have to start from that realization that what we're arguing about is a defensive barrier and not reality as such. It's a merely plausible estimate. My guru, Nitya, had a wonderful analogy. It's a little out of date now, but back in the last century many of us went to movie theaters. We'd sit and watch films projected on a screen. Nitya likened consciousness to the projecting light in a movie theater. The light shines through a film which contains various images and colors that change the bright white light of the projector into variegated colors and patterns and throws them on a screen on the wall. Our ego, or our conscious awareness, is like

LIBERATING OURSELVES

the people sitting in the chairs looking at the screen watching the show. We walked into the movie house as free people, but pretty soon we got so absorbed in what we were watching that we forgot the whole context and just became part of the movie.

That's really the position we're in now. We are absorbed in this movie we're watching. We don't even realize it's being played on the screen of our brain. It looks like it's "out there." And we certainly never turn around to look at the projector. If we were able to do that, we could see the source light that is making all that we see possible. We'd also get some idea of the film that is interfering with the light in a way to make it interesting, only no longer pure. The projection of light through the images on the film has many variations. It gets mixed with shadow. That's what makes life. Of course, it's a wonderful thing. But if we are only absorbed in the movie, then when someone is killed on screen, we're very sad and we cry. Or when the monster sneaks up out of the basement, we're terrified. When we're soaring on the back of a flying dragon, we're exhilarated. And so on. But, if we're really paying attention, we're really just yogis sitting in chairs.

So, to bring us back to our subject, we all believe in the projected images. Spiritualists, scientists and religious people all do the same thing and they all get drawn into and caught up in conflicts and absurdities because they, like we, have forgotten themselves. Everyone is in this position of being deluded and distracted by our own prejudices and peer pressures. As long as ten people agree with us then we're sure we're right. But that

CAN SCIENCE AND SPIRITUALITY EXIST?

actually is no ratification at all. They could all be wrong, and then we all end up buying into something delusory.

Nitya also spoke about another social phenomenon. If you look at history, you will see that ideas never last for very long. They come and go. They look really good for a while and then they are shown to be faulty, and something else replaces them. The odd thing, though, is that we always think right now we're right and everybody before us was wrong. But a wise person knows that next year there will be a new position, a new notion of what's right which may or may not be more or less absurd. So why not start with just thinking of these ideas as "provisional estimates." They are our "best guess" for the moment. We can put a lot of energy into understanding them, but we also know that they're bound to be a only partial assessment and that there is always going to be much more to learn.

The "G" Word

In the nineteenth century, the British Physical Society (and other groups) presumed that everything was known and that physical science was now closed. Max Planck, who originated quantum physics, was told in college not to become a physicist because that was all finished. There was nothing more to learn, so he was wasting his time becoming a physicist. Luckily, he persevered and opened up vast new realms. The history of our species is encountering vast new realms every time we think we have come to the end of something. This can't help but give us hope. It may actually be what has caused certain scientists to use the G word. The principle of emergent phenomena and evolutionary leaps could be called God, because it just keeps happening.

What is it about our universe that wonderful new things keep coming up? Obviously, God is a loaded term that people are willing to fight over, so maybe we should use a less loaded term like the Absolute. No matter what you call it, there's some inherent principle going on here that invites us to learn more and helps us to grow—if we are so inclined. And many of us are so inclined. Here's another short paragraph from one of the books by my guru, Nitya. It addresses the structure of consciousness and how we can apply spiritual wisdom into the practicalities of life:

> As a result of the conditioning of the faithful by the established religions, and of the skeptics by the categoric statements of science, man has become bifurcated in his sense of his true beingness. Having thus separated him from his true ground—that substratum that gives rise to all beings—those responsible for this have largely repressed in him the sense of wonder and delight in which one who knows his true being lives all the time. Looking in vain for some religious statement or scientific formula which will neatly encompass the whole mystery of being, so that we can file it away in our box of consumer goods and calendar maxims, we have forgotten that the mystery we seek to penetrate is our own mystery.

CAN SCIENCE AND SPIRITUALITY EXIST?

This matters. We should be full of wonder and delight, and yet we've somehow learned to seek simple formulas, sound bites or the right answers to questions. We're a bit like trained seals. We've spent so much time in school getting correct answers to questions that we think that somehow that's going to make us happy all by itself. This "correct answers" route is one of the problematic underpinnings of science. We're somehow convinced that if we get the right answer, everyone will love us and it will solve many problems and we'll all be happy.

I'm not saying that we shouldn't try to find the right answers to questions. I am saying that it's not the whole picture. It's just one aspect. There are so many other areas in which we need to allow ourselves to think, feel and be. It's in these areas that the wonder and delight of life resides.

Reintroducing Unity in Our Life

There is always a gap between a thing and how we comprehend it. Knowing that we have more to learn and that we can always add more to our understanding should be the measure of our humility. It's lack of humility and closed mindedness that causes conflict and parochialism. Getting the right answer gives a little jolt to the ego for a short time. But then that's over and we're back to being our old miserable selves. So we need to go beyond right answers.

LIBERATING OURSELVES

What we have to do in spiritual life is to allow the 99.9% of our intelligence that is not part of our conscious awareness to trickle back in and become part of our everyday understanding. It's an opening process. We tend to feel that defending ourselves with closed barriers of thoughts and words is going to keep us safe, but to really be everything we can be, which includes wonder and delight, we have to open up to that projector in us that is producing these movies of our lives which seem so coherent and full of amazing coincidences that it's hard to imagine they are completely random. Actually, they're not random, because our whole intelligence is working very hard to make our dimwitted consciousness knit together what's really going on. We have an expanding universe within our minds as well as what we see outside. We are both. And if we can harmonize both of those aspects of ourselves—the moviegoer and the visionary—then everyone will get along much better.

So I hope people don't feel that clinging to their preferred discipline, their specialty, is somehow where salvation lies. Instead it is best to have a broad contextual understanding and also be very good at your field of expertise. These must go together. If we live in isolation, we fear the other. We want to defend ourselves or fight with the other. But if we accept that we're all in the same situation as both moviegoers and visionaries, specialists and universal thinkers, we will realize the direness of our situation and we will become willing to pull together to embrace everyone before we are eradicated as a species.

CAN SCIENCE AND SPIRITUALITY EXIST?

Unity in Diversity

One of the great mysteries is that, despite the fact that we are all producing a stage show in our brains, there is significant coherence among people. Even though we're isolated individuals, there is actually something which allows us to communicate with each other. There's some connection. That's what a spiritual person taps into—that ground of unity. Jung called it the collective unconscious. And that's what we all spring from. So there is a unity within the diversity. And that is an important thing to recognize because diversity is the basis of conflict.

Diversity is what we can see, what we perceive. It's what our brain is attuned to showing us, because differences can be dangerous—lethal even. So we pay close attention to them. Because people believe what they see, many of them scoff at this notion of unity, of a common ground. They say, "We can't see it, so it's not there."

Scientists are often guilty of this divisive thinking. And yet, they are also currently the ones who are taking us into material proof of unity. An example is the human genome project. It proved beyond any reasonable doubt that the human race is one species. We now know that we're a family that probably started going its separate ways about 60,000 years ago, give or take 10,000. But before that, we were down to maybe less than 10,000 people.

LIBERATING OURSELVES

The human race was almost extinguished 60,000 years ago. But since then, we have spread all over the world. And in that time, a number of subtle variations have occurred. We take note of certain variations, and make a big fuss over them. As Nataraja Guru so poignantly said, we have to abandon the myth of the inferior or primitive human. We are all exactly this one species, one family. If we only look at the diversity and the differences, we will always have reasons to get upset and to argue and fight and eventually kill each other. But if we can realize that these people really are our cousins and that we came from the same little nest at the very tip of Africa, we will also realize our inherent unity, which will promote positive attitudes in working toward solutions to our problems. This, of course, is true on many levels.

In the nineteenth century, Christians and others were talking about the unity of humans. They said that we were all the same—all children of God. That's why the anti-slavery movement existed; it was a religious thing. It's hard to imagine now because it's turned around so completely. But the ideal vision, which is to see us all united at our core, is what liberates us and allows us to be very effective in solving problems.

Mirror neurons were discovered about 20 years ago. They are the neurons in our brain which, when someone else performs an action in front of us, perform the same action in our mind and reproduce it quite exactly. The most obvious example is when somebody yawns, we yawn. But on a neurological level, it's also happening, and this is the real basis of compassion and empathy.

CAN SCIENCE AND SPIRITUALITY EXIST?

We are not just pitying that sad person or injured person out there, we are feeling it inside ourselves. It is part of the processing that the brain is doing. I was thrilled when mirror neurons were discovered and presented to the world in science papers because their premise is very much central to the religious sentiments of loving and caring and compassion.

We are emerging from a dry intellectual period of blind watchmakers, desert sands of time, and dog eat dog and survival of the fittest. The compassionate, coherent working together within species or among species is becoming central to our understanding of evolution and who we are. In fact, we not only have to give up the myth of the inferior or primitive man, we need to give it up regarding all creatures. We have considered animals to be dumb, so we could exploit them and mistreat them in all sorts of ways. But another encouraging trend of science is the realization that this disregard for animal experience was, in fact, was a projection. It was our own film over the truth, our own coloration of truth. The more we look at animals without this lens, we realize how amazing, brilliant, compassionate, empathetic and wonderful they are. Not to mention flat out smart. It's encouraging to see this happening. People are starting to get a little uncomfortable about the things we've been doing to animals for thousands of years based on seeing only differences and masking our mirror neurons. We *feel* that animals know pain and suffering, yet, until now, we haven't allowed ourselves to believe it. I'm happy that's beginning to turn around.

LIBERATING OURSELVES

The Mystery of Change

One of the things that baffles me most is how positive change takes place. What is it that draws a person to explore who they are instead of just accepting what they are told and carrying on as if it didn't matter? And how do leaps of understanding take place? It's really interesting to ponder. It's a mystery. There is no formula I can give, but I can point out that there's a sweep of history that's very coherent. We can see this in our personal lives too. If you look back at your life, what seemed to be a series of jumbled decisions and chaos has a real coherency to it. We developed in a certain way, we developed certain strengths, and we have been given opportunities to use those strengths to develop ourselves to this point. Some invisible factor —I don't even want to name it —is behind this thing that we all tap into. We're just one dot in the picture, and the picture includes all of this.

How does change evolve in a very unified way through different stages? How did that happen in European music for example? Why does the end of Mozart sound exactly like the beginning of Beethoven? Calculus was invented in two separate places, by Leibnitz and Newton, at the same instant. I guess there were others who laid down the groundwork for both of them, but the fully formed calculus came out at the same time in two different places. That's not uncommon. So I think we can feel that there is a tide of history in which we are both little specks and important players. Sometimes it's terrifying. It's often terrifying, but we should also be filled with wonder and admiration that this is happening. We are being invited to play our part.

Finally, if the universe were based on our understanding, it would have crashed and burned a long time ago. Luckily, we don't have to understand it. We don't have to answer all the questions perfectly in order for the universe to continue to function in its beautiful organic unified fashion. No matter what we believe, we are carried by the tide—we are part of the vast universal organism. So, lets revel in it. Let's share with our neighbors how wonderful it is to be part of this unique and spectacular tide of life. It should give us reason to love and be happy, rather than to be fearful and depressed. The idea is that we all, atheist and theist alike, have a highest value. There is some level of stability. We can feel it, we can visualize it and we can move towards it. It is the goal of spiritual life and it is also the goal of science.

3

Freeing a Whale Caught in Nets

The Entertainment Trap

There's so much entertainment and amusement in our culture that most people feel like they just need a new entertainment and they'll be amused and that's all life is about. We just go from one amusing thing to the next and that's life.

Fortunately there's something inside of us whose longing is much more profound than entertainment can satisfy. We came to be born to actualize some incredible potentials lying latent in our genetics and possibly other places. Scientists are finding new avenues through which information from the past can be transmitted to the present. We're full of potentials, and what happens in the course of becoming a socialized human being is that those potentials are suppressed and we're given alternative versions of ourselves. These "alternative versions" are, in most cases, not very expressive. Some of us do better than others of course. But I think we all are distracted from our potentials to some degree, and we learn to accept this as the normal condition, so those potentials, which are really agitating to become actualized, just sit inside us and fester.

We can keep ourselves distracted for a long time with various entertainments, but sooner or later this starts to corrode our psyche and damage our persona. The persona is not a solid thing; it's a supposition. It is a strategy devised by an infant to cope with environmental demands. When it starts falling apart we either become desperate to find out who we are, or else struggle to maintain the illusion. Society is oriented to maintaining the illusion. That's where the entertainment comes in. That's where the medications, legal and illegal, come in. We just medicate ourselves so that we don't notice that we're not able to be our full selves. We accept these socially imposed restrictions and go meekly to our demise. Thoreau, who was an American yogi, said that most people live lives of quiet desperation. That expresses it very well. We follow the dictates of our surroundings and we meekly try to behave accordingly, but we're really desperate because none of it satisfies us deep down.

Freeing a Whale

There's a wonderful video that I saw on YouTube. Millions of other people have seen it too. A small group of concerned citizens in a boat in a bay in Baja, California come upon what looks like a dead humpback whale. They sit in the boat wondering what could have happened to this amazing, gigantic creature that is just lying there. And suddenly, the whale exhales and takes in a huge breath. They realize it's not dead at all. It's immobile. But it's alive.

After thinking it over for a while, one of the people swims over to it and realizes that the whale is caught in fishing nets and is completely bound up in them and will certainly die soon if nothing is done. Gathering their courage, these people try to cut the nets away. They work for quite a while. It's really a struggle. But the nets come off and eventually the last net slides off the tail and the whale is free. It starts to swim away and they assume that's the end of the story. We saved the whale and it's gone. But then the whale starts leaping in the air and slapping its tail and just frolicking in the ocean. The exuberance of being alive is transmitted so beautifully by this animal that it's really a wonder to watch.

As I watched the video, I realized this is our situation too. The fishing nets that we're caught in are the social constraints and conditionings that are laid onto us from birth. And pretty soon, as we grow, we're very close to being immobilized by them. The point of a spiritual endeavor is to take the nets off. It's to free ourselves again. It must be a conscious decision: should I meekly remain bound and be a good, well-adjusted member of society, or do I want reclaim that sense of freedom that really is who I am? If I decide to reclaim my freedom, it's going to take some efforts, first to recognize how I'm caught, and then to strip those nets off. There are various types of nets, and I will talk about those as we go along. The category we're going to treat first is assumptions and expectations.

Assumptions and Expectations

The drama of humans cutting the whale free of its nets is a lovely metaphor, but in this story the whale is helpless to get the nets off by itself. It is completely dependent on someone coming along and setting it free. But we humans actually have the ability to participate in our own liberation, in getting free of the nets. Certainly, in most cases, we do need help. Very few people (Narayana Guru was one) did it completely on their own. Most of us need guidance. But we also have to participate. I'm afraid that the savior syndrome that permeates our culture teaches us that we're helpless and that someone else should come along and save us. But in Vedanta philosophy, in healthy Indian philosophy, we are participants. We have hands—we can pull the nets off. This isn't about someone else doing it for us: this is about us accomplishing a miracle.

Let me first make a distinction between expectations and assumptions. In the psychological sense of the term, expectations are conscious and assumptions are unconscious. Most of the nets which entrap us can be classified as assumptions. They are the things that we learn early on and become adjusted to and consider as the very structure of the world we live in. Based on those assumptions, we develop a number of expectations about what's going to happen if we do this or someone or something else does that. That's the conscious aspect of this dilemma. Both of them are important. The *Bhagavad Gita* is famous for advising us to stop having expectations. It's a preliminary teaching, but it's very important, and in that work it is elaborated upon in depth.

The idea is that because they're conscious, our expectations are accessible to us. We should be able to visualize them very easily: I do something and I expect something in return. Casting off our expectations is spiritual advice. In the world of transactions, expectations are valid. If you work all week, you should expect a paycheck on Friday. If the paycheck's not there, there's a problem and you have to deal with that. It is a conscious shaping of a situation based upon an implied contract. I'm going to talk a lot about the contractual basis of our thinking as one of our key assumptions. I'll get to that a little later, but we really expect if we do X, we'll get Y in return. That type of thinking permeates our culture. Unfortunately it permeates our spiritual thinking, too.

On the other hand, if I ask my friend to do something, I understand that they may or may not do it, so I relinquish that implied contractual expectation. It frees me from potential disappointment and it frees the other person from an obligation to me that they may not even know they have. We can accomplish a lot by witnessing and moderating our expectations. We may still expect something is going to happen. We just don't know what it is. We become more open to what's going to happen because we don't pin it down to one small area.

The really deep nets and conditionings that we suffer from are the assumptions. Assumptions are the way we have been raised to view the world. We are so accustomed to it being a certain way, we don't even notice how we are shaping it.

Expectations and assumptions are known to skew scientific experiments. Somewhere in the mid twentieth century, people began to notice that their experiments were coming up with the results that the administrators of the experiments had hoped to demonstrate. And they realized that actually, there's a mystical, mysterious connection between our conscious expectations and our unconscious assumptions and how the experiments turn out. So the double-blind was designed. In the double blind experiments, the people administering the experiments didn't even know what was going on. In many cases, they didn't even know what the experiment was. They certainly didn't know who was getting what medicine or who was in what group, and so on. It was a very important step in research. It is the scientific way of cutting out expectations and assumptions. If we want to access truth in ourselves by bringing out what is authentic within us, then we have to find a way to eliminate both the expectations we have accumulated and the assumptions that have been conditioned into us.

Assumptions underlie our entire social structure. They are so deeply woven into the fabric of social order and individual thought that we don't even recognize them. What we have to do to begin to see them is to sit quietly as spiritual beings and

LIBERATING OURSELVES

look at ourselves as individuals. And as we do that, we tease out and begin to see certain assumptions that make us prejudiced. We may not believe it now, but inside us, those assumptions and beliefs are lurking and twisting our outlook. And unless we sit down and say "Aha, there it is! That's how it's affecting me. I want to give that up," they're just going to stay inside and continue to distort our perceptions.

One assumption that has been conditioned into us is that humans are born sinners. Even those of us who are not a part of the religious background of the West assume that children are ignorant brutes who need to be disciplined and re-formed in order to become worthy adults. Unconsciously, we well-intentioned adults, who are bound up in our own nets, apply this point of view to our child rearing, so kids grow up feeling there's something wrong with them, that they're not good enough, or don't measure up. Note that this attitude feeds exactly right into our consumer based culture, which promises products to make us better and more likable.

The result of this assumption is that children develop low self-esteem. Subject to constant re-formation and discipline, the ego core in the child starts to build defenses. This defense system becomes a persona—the personality. It's the strategy the child develops to cope with a hostile environment. What do I do so that I stop getting yelled at? Or stop getting hit? Or get my food on time? What do I do to get attention? I obviously can't just be me.

FREEING A WHALE CAUGHT IN NETS

I'm not good enough as I am, so here's what I'll do… I'll become this.

The development of personality is the beginning of the child's leaving its true self. Society praises it as the maturing process, and maybe it *is* something the child has to do. But as adults, it's something we may want to undo. It is a strategy that was devised by a barely conscious little creature. As adults, we can bring understanding to that unconscious area of defense and bluster and fakery. We no longer need it. We're not children defending ourselves against gigantic, manipulative beings anymore. We can drop the nets. We can be free.

There are so many of these nets, and they are individual in the way they are experienced and expressed. My mother believed that little babies should be left to cry; it was good for their lung development. But all my life, I have battled feelings of inadequacy, of being unwanted. I trace them back to being left to cry in infancy. When I really wanted the thing that I loved most, it would not come to me. My mother could have come to me but she just didn't. It was arbitrary. I suspect that I sensed I wasn't lovable enough for my mother to come over and feed me. It was that basic. I was a sentient being and I was hurt. I was miserably hurt. That's why I cried. And then all those things became a layer of despair and valuelessness that impeded my life in a number of ways.

So now, when those feelings pop up in social interactions with people I love, I recognize them and I say, "Oh, there's that the thing from the crib." I recognize that these are not current feelings that I'm having toward my friend. No. They are a memory leaping up into my present experience out of a past association. If I don't recognize the root of the feelings, I might think "My friend doesn't like me. I don't matter to them," which might damage an otherwise good relationship with someone who actually does love me. So it's my job to throw this old association, this net, out. Then I can have a more wonderful relationship with my friend because I'm not holding on to this burden from the past.

Recently I have been working with somebody who's falling apart as a result of a network of unconscious assumptions. For him and for all of us, this is life and death stuff. That whale is going to die if we don't take the nets off.

The assumption that he is an inadequate person and a sinner makes him think he can't solve his own problems; somebody else has to. This goes so deep in many of our lives. Sit down and think. Do I really deep down believe that I am not able to solve my own problems? This very strong conviction has to be countermanded or it will stay there and paralyze us—just like the whale caught in the net.

Many of us, like this friend of mine, are in crisis and really need therapy, but we don't go. Something in us resists. I realized one reason for this. As students, we were endlessly tested in school, and we came to understand that these tests were markers of our success or failure in life. When taking tests we were told that getting outside help was cheating. The message we learned was "Getting help is cheating." This is a common net—one that prevents us from entering into exactly the kind of conversations with skilled professionals that will help us get free.

In fact, the whole testing thing, even without the cheating part, is based on deferring our sense of worth to some outside measuring stick that's being foisted on us. Somehow the belief that a judgmental god is watching over us has transmuted itself into so many things, including testing, spying and monitoring everything.

So, in the test taking metaphor, you're on your own. Getting help is cheating. You stand or fall by whether you get the right answer. Here's another aspect of this: Many people feel if they get the wrong answer, they have failed. But neuroscience now is telling us that the brain learns by making mistakes and then adjusting to them. So making mistakes is actually the way to learn. At least it's an important feature. So the fear of making mistakes and the blocking out of making mistakes is actually impeding the learning process. It's actually counterproductive.

This fear goes with us into adulthood. Lurking in the back of our minds is "If I don't do this right, I'm a failure or something awful will happen." Who needs that weight? We can throw it off. We can all laugh about it. We make a silly mistake. So what? It's hilarious. We didn't expect that. That's great. We can correct it. No problem. We don't need to operate according to the old assumptions. If we begin to see them, we can begin to be free of them.

LIBERATING OURSELVES

Another net is the deferral of authority to other people. We think that somewhere else people are making decisions that really matter and we don't matter, and that just fosters the sense of not really being worthwhile. But, this net is relatively easy to escape. Here's an excellent technique. When you think of someone as an authority figure, you can cancel it with the simultaneous understanding that we are all just people, that we're all just works in progress, people doing the best we can. None of us has the full story. The authorities' claims that they have the full story are based on fallible laws and premises.

When I worked in the fire department, we got a new fire chief who was a hellfire and brimstone guy who was going to change everything. No more fun around the firehouse. We were going to work hard and earn every penny. He terrorized the entire department. He said, "All our lieutenants and captains will be coming to me for 2-hour meetings, and we'll get my new program going here." People spent weeks dreading their impending meetings. You could see them walking around with pale, drawn and miserable faces. Then they'd go for their meeting and the chief would rant at them and they'd come home with their tail between their legs and tell us, "We've got to change everything we do. Enough of this sitting around and chatting with each other and having fun. We've got to work, work, work."

Everybody was unhappy, so I said to myself, "You know, this is just a guy. I want to have a meeting with him." I was not an officer. I was at the bottom of the heap. Everybody thought I was crazy. But eventually I got my appointment and I went in and just treated this man like a fellow human being. I didn't treat him like a chief. I didn't have any false respect. I did not acknowledge that I was an underling and that he was an over ling. We were on the same level. Because I wasn't cowering in the shadows, I was able to see all of the ploys he was trying to lay on me to convince me of his position. And in the end, he responded to my technique in a very positive way. I think he was relieved to not be put into the position of exaggerated authority, and we had a wonderful, fruitful talk.

Because I didn't acquiesce to his authority, the chief and I had a very enjoyable interchange. We actually accomplished some positive things. I was able to request a few things that he then implemented. We can do this kind of work in all areas of our lives.

In order to make this kind of progress, a meditative practice, a contemplative practice, sitting down and really thinking about how you view the world and what that means, is incredibly instructive and valuable. It is a way to separate out the assumptions we live by when we are unconscious about the truth of a current situation. There's nothing simple about this work. It is not an entertainment or distraction. It's not some kind of psychedelic or artistic experience that accidentally and temporarily breaks us free of our nets. It takes hard work and doesn't happen by accident. Changing ourselves requires rewiring our brains. A new kind of thinking can accomplish this. It is the science of self-realization and it is worth talking about.

I recently had an interesting insight. People talk about taking a drug and getting high and then returning to the place they were before they got high, as if that experience doesn't mean anything or has no value. Knowing that there's an alternative consciousness, an ocean we could be frolicking in instead of sitting here bummed out at our desks, is enlightening in itself. Part of the education of that kind of experience is that you don't stay in that ocean. You are brought back to exactly where you were sitting when you left because that's where you need to work. That's what needs to be transformed. You. The place you're working from. The ocean is always there. We are part of it. We are creatures that live in that ocean. But we are also bound and seriously stuck, and that's exactly where we have to work.

For some reason, we want to ignore the stuck place and be as far away from it as possible. But until we get right into it and work there, we don't grow adequately. We must learn to not say, "Let's escape again," but instead to say, "Oh, let's transform this place right here where we are."

Using Intelligence to Free Ourselves

I realize that it is an unpopular position to believe that we can think our way out of the boxes we are in. Even in the video, the whale is at the mercy of other people to free it. It seems counterintuitive that we can use thinking to free ourselves because thinking is very much connected to the nets, the conditioning and the bondage that we're in. The thoughts that oppress us are repetitive and infuriating. We think of the little voice in our head as our thoughts. Like a radio station, it broadcasts a compilation of the input we've recorded in our life, good, bad and indifferent. A lot of it is pretty bad and inappropriate. In a way, it's the voice of society speaking to us. It's like our superego, our learned mental capabilities, trying to discipline the rest of us to fall into line, stay put, and be well-adjusted.

There is a lot of science (real methodologies) in the Indian tradition that shows us how we can—often with the help of others, but even on our own—use our intelligence to free ourselves. It's an entirely different way of using the mind that's creative and dynamic. Restraining the controlling centers of the ego allows our full being to participate in our life. But once we stop making the effort, then our habitual perspective returns. Because that's the way our brains are wired. We can't immediately change that, even if we have a vision of what needs to change. We need to foster a new open position through mental discipline in order that we may hold back our immediate reactions. This is particularly hard because we tend to believe in our reactions. An overriding belief in the value of potentials needs to come to the forefront of our thinking.

Here I'm going to talk about the yoga of dialectics. If you suppress your natural reactions, it's like you've taken off the pressure-relief valve of a steam boiler so the pressure builds up in the unconscious until there's an explosion. Suppression is not a good technique. It doesn't work. But "annulment" does. Zen, for instance, is an attempt to bypass suppression by becoming ecstatically engaged in something different. The "something different" is energized by forms of thinking. In fact, the word "Zen" comes from *dhyanam* in Sanskrit, which means meditation or contemplation. The word changed as it went east into China and Japan, but it's the same concept. It's meditation. We think of the insight as arriving like an intense burst of lightning. But there are many ways to disrupt our bondage.

This leads me to bring up the core assumption that we are all in thrall to. We assume that what we see and perceive is reality because what we picture in our mind is so convincing and so realistic that we believe it is the form reality takes. Yet that is not true. Neuroscientists are coming to realize this from their studies also. This is something the rishis have known for thousands of years. What scientists are coming to understand now is that what we are actually perceiving is an immense jumble of vibrations that have very little feature to them. It's like being in a blizzard, basically. And maybe even a blizzard at night.

Yet out of this incredible cacophony of vibrations, our amazingly brilliant brain fashions a coherent picture that it presents as reality. Actually, this is probably the first and greatest miracle of our lives. We believe that we look out into a world and see what it is, and then base what we do on that. But it turns out that the impressions we're working with are created by us, and are based on prejudiced learning that is actually being generated, in part at least, by all the conditioning that we've undergone. This is why people of different ethnic groups, for instance, might look more frightening than people from our own group . We can unlearn these things, but the natural tendency of the projecting brain is to look at differences as probable threats.

What we're seeing is an illusion. That's not a bad thing. It's a wonderful, helpful illusion. It's often called maya, meaning our inevitably limited interpretation of reality. I use the term maya rather glibly, as though everyone knows what it means, but actually it's one those terms, like yoga, that is widely misunderstood. Maya is mistakenly understood to be the illusion that hides reality, but in fact maya is the whole picture. The whole universe is maya. The amazing fact that something arose from nothing is maya. We humans attempt to overcome our illusions with insight and a maximum amount of input and sharing of information. For this reason alone, maya is a wonderful thing. It's not a curse. But included in the desire to really "know" reality must be the recognition that we have a long way to go to be fully aware of our inner and outer self.

Working with assumptions is a process. Each of us must find the assumptions undergirding our attitudes. We need to work with our own, not someone else's, problems. It's so much easier to criticize someone else! Forget them. We must constantly remind ourselves that we're in the midst of a reality that includes our own assumptions. Thinking and non-thinking can be brought together in an effort to see what's beyond us.

Here's how this awareness helps. When an assumption surfaces, when you begin to see it, don't foster it, don't support it. Instead say, "Okay, I'm done with that. That illusory assumption had me—I was caught—but now I'm going to stop. I don't want to be caught anymore. I absolutely relinquish being caught." And the assumption will keep coming back, but the fact that you have done this once means that you'll see it more quickly the next time and the next time and the next, and eventually it will lose its power, as you ease out of its grasp.

An excellent meditation opens you to the realization that there is more to life than what you have been seeing—that what you've been seeing is not everything. It can be a terrifying thing if you sit down and ponder it and come to realize that the world as you know it is a fiction that you've been generating for yourself. It's actually quite unnerving. It's like jumping into a black hole or something. So approach this kind of work with caution. Try not to lose yourself in it. And remember what I said earlier. The light that we presume is outside of us does not go in through the eyes into the brain to light up the world that we see. It's completely dark in the brain. All of the light that we see is generated by us from inside of ourselves. This is just astonishing. We are the light. We are the source of light. We are the visual, physical light, as well as the spiritual, intuitive light. We are the light of insight. It's all coming from inside.

It is important that we maintain some distance between the mental process and its culmination in thought. Otherwise, there would be no reason to change, no reason for us to suspect that we're actually millions of times more complex that we imagine we are. Remember those scientists using functional MRIs to observe brains in operation? They saw that the thought process originates in different areas that are deep in the brain. Through an unconscious process, the material that will become a thought gets batted around, travels here and there, and combines different areas. At the very tail end of this long process of development, something appears in the conscious arena, and we say, "I just thought of something," or, "This is what I see here; this is what I know," when in fact it's being handed to us, and we're just ratifying it.

Religious sentiments of worship and awe also come from these deep recesses within ourselves, but they highlight an interesting interplay between inner and outer information. We may think we're outwardly praying to some deity, but that deity is also part of the reflection of our unconscious being presented to our conscious mind. It may be a very great fiction, but it gives us the sense of reverence that is such an important aspect of a happy life. It tunes us in to something true and wonderful inside us. And we begin to observe what we already intuit—that what is "out there" is "in here."

I have a favorite quote about this from paleontologist/philosopher Teilhard de Chardin: "The history of the living world

LIBERATING OURSELVES

can be summarized as the elaboration of ever more perfect eyes within a cosmos in which there is always something more to be seen." While I have given a wordy explanation of why thinking and non-thinking are both important, I have wanted to emphasize that the thoughts that bother you, the thoughts that keep distracting you from something better, are worthy of being addressed and dismissed. Don't lump all thinking together, because there are some very subtle and excellent ways through which we can orient ourselves to a new kind of seeing and thinking that will open us up to a greater part of ourselves so that we might better come to know the ocean that's flowing within us at all times.

4

How Yoga Helps Us Break Free

What is "well adjusted," really?

Like the whale caught in the net, we can adjust to being snarled in all sorts of complicated requirements, necessities and obligations. We can adjust quite well to many situations. We can be people who withstand a violation of our natural state of mind and body without too much apparent discomfort. Ironically, those of us who can suffer those indignities are called "well adjusted" people. Yet "well adjusted" people are often the ones who commit the high crimes and misdemeanors—not the low crimes of stealing a loaf of bread, but the things that can lead an entire society off the edge of a cliff. Needless to say, well adjusted is a problematic term.

What happens to the psyche when we become well adjusted to a condition of bondage is that our innate urge for freedom does not die with it. It is suppressed, and it is always trying to rise to the surface. If it's unable to do so, then what happens is that we turn to a fantasy life. We substitute an imaginary world of the mind for the world of nature and natural phenomena. Our fantasies easily become bizarre extrapolations that prompt war, hate, contention, anxiety, and terror. These things are not healthy even as fantasies, and our imagination follows them into some really horrific places. It's no wonder then that the world is beset with conflicts everywhere. Consider the types of fantasies that we have. Look at our movies and video games. It is one thing to rectify, purify or refine those fantasies to make them nicer—the task of a Sisyphus. But the real cure is in breaking free from the state of bondage. Then we become naturally disinclined to the violence and meanness of spirit that we see around us.

The key thrust of Vedanta philosophy, as expressed in the *Bhagavad Gita* for example, is to re-attain that state of freedom from conditioning. Trying to refine our fantasies and behavior to make them nicer and better is an infinite game, a never-ending process. We cannot make incremental steps to achieve a total change of paradigm. We must make a breakthrough to return to a state of freedom. It's the only way to become a liberated human being. Most of the practices to attain liberation are of the incremental type, which demands a lot of work and requires that each blockage is addressed separately. It makes sense, but it takes forever. It's also something you do in lieu of making a breakthrough, another kind of distraction.

A commonly accepted fantasy is that we can't break free from our blockages. Our culture seems to have a stake in everyone staying bound and committed to feeding their energy into the established pocketbooks. But we don't have to participate in that. The alternative is yoga. Yoga is the way to break out of our condition of bondage in a wholesale, not piecemeal, manner. Let's move on to Yoga Dialectics as a healing art.

Of course, there's a polite version of yoga that has taken root in the West and is well accepted and glibly spoken of. But the yoga I'm talking about is not hatha yoga. Hatha yoga is one very small part of yoga philosophy that has to do with calming the body so that your thinking is not tied to it, but is free to wander where it will, like our whale. We do have a lot of demands of the body. Some of them are just cosmetic and some of them are more health-oriented. And hatha yoga deals with those very nicely.

The yoga I'm talking about is the philosophy of yoga as a liberating tool of our intelligence. It boils down to a very simple proposition. Yoga means yoking. It means joining together. The proposition is that there's a unifying factor or a unity underlying all aspects of the world that we live in. Unfortunately we see it as broken into bits because our brain is designed to treat individual aspects of that unity in isolation, assess their threat or benefit potential, and respond to them on that basis. It's fine as far as it goes, but it keeps us grounded in what we call horizontal activity, which is tied to the transactional world around us. If we want to liberate ourselves, though, we must introduce a different dimension, a vertical dimension. In this vertical dimension lies our expansive, evolutionary potential as human beings.

In order to awaken our potential, we need to re-access the unity underlying all of the apparently separate aspects of the world and tie them together. It sounds exotic I suppose, but is quite simple in essence. In practice, it's a challenge, but it's easy enough to make a start because the approach is simple. The ancient Greeks used a form of dialectics in which two opposing arguments, a thesis and an antithesis, were juxtaposed. When these were considered intelligently it resulted in an insight that was greater than either the thesis or the antithesis by itself. They called this insight the synthesis, a unifying understanding that is greater than the sum of its parts. From that point of view one was able to see, understand, include and even reconcile the thesis and antithesis.

That's essentially what yoga is. Yoga is the Sanskrit word for dialectics in the ancient Greek sense. There are many types of dialectics, but this simple, essential one is just fine for our purposes. Let's stick to just a proposition (thesis) and its opposite (antithesis), and treat them as belonging to one, rather than two, contexts. I'll give some examples of how this works.

Good vs. Bad

Good and bad are rigidly defined in our personal, educational and social training, and we all develop a persona that we claim or hold to be good. We're taught to be good, and the types of thinking or behavior that don't fit with our notion of good are considered bad. Because of this we form a black and white picture of good and bad. But there is no absolute good or bad. Good and bad are relative positions that are based on each other.

What we need to do is to get out of thinking in terms of good as opposed to bad and start thinking in terms of unitive activity. This thought generally horrifies people because they're so grounded in being good. I suppose in a fantasy world taking sides might work, because if it was true that good and bad are not related and had no common ground, then, sure, let's fight for good and destroy the evil and that will be that. But the truth is that good and bad *are* connected.

Good and bad are like a coin with a heads and a tails. I defy you to come up with a one-sided coin. In a manifested universe, you don't have one-dimensional coins. Good and bad are joined. So if we emphasize the good and we work really hard for it and do lots of good things, it seems really admirable and praiseworthy. But we have a shadow of that, that's growing commensurately. The bad grows equally with the good because they are not two different things. They are parts of the same coin, so all of our efforts to do good are simultaneously augmenting the bad.

What do you do about it? Some people say, "Well, I should just be bad, and then that will augment the good." But the problem is that neither of these is a true proposition. Good and bad are not part of the natural order. They are constructions that we have made in our minds to distinguish things. And they have an operational value, of course. But, what we want to do as yogis is to access that unitive state from which good and bad emerge. We have to intelligently bring those together, dialectically.

LIBERATING OURSELVES

Here is an example. Cruelty and compassion can be a thesis and antithesis. We want to be compassionate to other people. We think that we will resolve all of our problems if we're nice to each other. And yet, there are all these mean people around. What do we do about that? Well, we could reject the mean people or put them in jail or treat them as inferior and not care about them. There's a whole range of ways that we express disdain for the "bad" people of the world. But a yogi would do something different. He would ask, "What has brought this situation about?" He would look at the actual conditions of the people who are considered bad, and would begin to see the logic of how they came to be what they are. He would see that circumstances, training, lack of opportunities, abuse, or a host of other conditions are what led these "bad" people into this position.

And he would have compassion for that situation. It doesn't mean that he would be endorsing crime or anything like that. Instead, he would be letting go of the polarized thinking of "this side is right and that side is wrong." He would also notice how a punitive approach rebounds to cause a host of ills for "good" people too. He would realize that polarized thinking is what causes so much grief. The really wise seers of the world embrace everyone. The average person has a tough time with that, but the principle of yoga shows us how to get to that. It can't be a phony position, like "Everybody's okay, and we'll leave it at that." It has to be *realized*. It has to come be known deep inside of us that we all have our pluses and minuses, our gifts and faults, and that we're all in the same position.

HOW YOGA HELPS US BREAK FREE

Imagine that you experienced the upbringing, incidents and accidents of each and every person. With that knowledge, no matter how much you might despise a person, you would come to see that, if you had gone through those same situations, you would probably have come out exactly like them. Nurturing easily overrides genetic inheritance. Biologically we could be very similar to those people that we think are so terrible. It's just that our conditions were different. It's the situation that causes the problem. Knowing that reorients our entire psyche from hatred and rejection to understanding and even insight into what could rectify the situation.

That's what real yoga does. It doesn't give you a more flexible body. It gives you a more flexible mind. And the more you embrace yoga, the more you liberate yourself. Through yoga, you not only let go of the other person, you let go of the hatred that's lurking inside you. I heard a speaker quoting Soltzhenitsyn the other day. He said that it would be wonderful if we could put a big thick dividing line between the good people and the bad people. But the problem is that the line would go right down the middle of each of us. To accept the good and bad in all of us—especially ourselves—is an evolutionary leap forward that we should all be making.

Remember, as fearful children, our strategy was, "We'll be good and then bad things won't happen to us. We won't be hurt. We won't be spanked. We won't be humiliated. So we're going to put our efforts into being good and not bad." That perverted our psyches. It was a well motivated, well intentioned strategy that we developed for our protection, but it wound up tying us in knots and isolating us or alienating us from our true inner potential. It created some of the nets that bind us. To reclaim our true inner potential we have to step outside of that kind of juvenile, polarizing thinking to something better, something that will allow for synthesis and understanding, something that will actually set us free.

Okay vs. Not Okay

The next most important way we can apply yoga dialectics is to understand that this obsession with good and bad has made us think of ourselves as being okay or not okay. Even though the truth is that we are both okay and not okay at any given moment and that we all have good and bad qualities, our society can make us feel inadequate, unloved, unwelcome, and uniformly not okay.

I have a motto: "Self description is stultifying." The more we think of ourselves as this or that, the more we stay stuck in that position. We become tied down to something that we're not. In consequence we become stupid. When we were growing up, our caregivers encouraged us to define ourselves. We were told to "know who you are, define it, lay claim to it, accept responsibility for everything you do." All of these injunctions prompted us to construct a persona that we can use as a shield to reflect those values. Underneath the "I'm okay" persona, the feeling is, "I'm not okay." We have this shield that says we're okay. And secretly, down inside, we feel like we're not okay, because we know perfectly well we don't match the "okay" image. It's like our clothing. It's just something we put on and off. It's not really us. So we're really not okay. But we're fooling everybody else quite successfully. And for the moment, that is okay.

I suggest that we abandon stultifying self-descriptions. Let's stop being fixated on what we are and who we are and how good we are and how okay or not okay we are, and instead just be what we are. But to get over it we can't simply say, "I don't believe in that stuff anymore." Like the netting that trapped the whale, self-description doesn't just go away when we stop believing in it. Phillip K. Dick's definition of reality is great. He says, "Reality is that which, when you stop believing in it, doesn't go away." So unfortunately, the bondage that we're in is not a fantasy bondage. It's a real thing. And we need to peel it off intelligently. That's what we do as yogis. For that matter, that's what we do as adults. We recognize our obsession and fear around the issues of who we are, and we see that it is a diversion, an obstacle, that prevents us from diving into our deepest capacity and bringing forth and expressing our best qualities.

Let's *do* that. Let's try to express our best qualities. How can we do that? We can start by trying to express things and see what happens. Unfortunately, very often the things we try are just more conditioning. They're what we've heard is "okay." We have a collection of opinions based on our concepts of good and bad, and we hold on to them very tightly. Everybody wants to be an artist, for example, because that symbolizes freedom. But there's a little more to it than just thinking you're an artist. This is what meditation is for: to recognize that these ideas are not absolute truths. They are our opinions and our prejudices. We need to notice them. By actually recognizing them, we can then counteract them with the opposite. Take racism for example. We may have been trained to think of people who are different than we are as inferior and dangerous. This training starts to be felt on a visceral level until it becomes wired into us. Our job must be to recognize it and come up with a countervailing response such as, "Oh, there it is again. I know it's not true even if something in me is attached to it." Then we must bring the two thoughts together: "Okay, I feel fear, but I know this is not a situation that's fear-inducing. It is just my own prejudice." Now, we're no longer blaming the other person for causing fear in us. We're seeing it coming up as part of our own conditioning, and we're negating what is fearful by embracing it. The real physical, tangible cure is that when something makes us afraid, we meet it. In this way, the fantasies that cause the fear are dissolved by the wonder and joy of true contact.

My family had an idea that if something happened that hurt you, you should immediately do it again. If you didn't, you developed a fear that you would lead you to always avoid it. If you were swimming and you swallowed a bunch of water and choked, you would be encouraged to go right back into the pool so you'd realize that the pool itself was not a hostile place. By going back in the pool, you'd immediately feel the delight of being there and come to understand that you had a small accident that was now over. So a single incident didn't become a fixed conditioning factor.

In general, if you fall off a horse, say, try to get right back on. If you skin your knee from running, get up and run again. Don't let mishaps become fixed conditioning factors. Don't let people feed your fear. Counteract fear intelligently. The more you do that, the more you access the free part of yourself that doesn't respond to fear or depend on opinions.

Being Alert to Mental Posturing

Yoga practice is really about being alert to our mental posturing, so we can offset it with an opposite proposition. It's only when we're in a consequent neutral position that we're free to go where the vagaries of fate or divine guidance or luck or the wonderful joy of being alive can lead us. If we're neutral, we're open to that guidance and free to go with it. If we're prejudiced, fixed, holding on, we resist and we miss so many opportunities.

It's a widely held belief that if you focus on the bad, then you're making it happen, so many people want to stay positive. I think that's another extrapolation of a childish mentality. There's fear behind it. Something that really bothers me is that spiritual groups are supposed to be only positive. Actually the idea is to be only unitive. That would embrace everything. Narayana Guru

LIBERATING OURSELVES

is a shining example of someone who embraced all people—the downtrodden and the alcoholic people as well as the healthy and well-heeled people. Having come from a low caste—the toddy tappers, the people who made coconut liquor in South India—he understood the artificiality of the spectrum. He had a way of embracing everyone without in any way endorsing sordid behaviors. His was the best example of a "universal embrace" that I've ever seen.

All of the really amazing saintly people have that ability to embrace a situation as it is and bring into it an oceanic sense of compassion and acceptance that is actually transformative. It heals the ills that cause people to do terrible things to themselves and others. It heals despair based on inadequate understanding and inadequate opportunities. And it brings understanding and opportunity for liberation to those places. In no way did Narayana Guru or the other great people of history ignore problems. Jesus was fairly famous for wading right into the places where the downtrodden were really suffering.

There's something askew if we only talk about sweetness and light. Of course the world is miraculous and wonderful, but it's miraculous and wonderful as a dual proposition in which one lion's good meal is another creature's demise. Interpretations of good and bad depend on points of view and other external factors. When we lean on the good and reject the bad, we actually tie ourselves in knots and bind ourselves more because we're afraid to accept that other side. It's almost like we have a posthypnotic suggestion to avoid bad things because of our dread of punishment.

This fear of the bad is an assumption that's lodged so deeply in our psyche we don't often recognize it. It takes dedicated meditation to start to see it in ourselves. But once we do, it starts to lose its grip on us. We become comfortable with the fact that the world includes a wide range of behaviors. If an abstract god or principle created the world, it might have thought, "I'll create a universe where there's only good things and where nothing bad ever happens." But as you can see, that didn't occur, basically because it's impossible. Whenever something is manifested it has a top and a bottom, it has a right and a left, a thesis and an antithesis. It can't be helped. It's the nature of manifestation.

So in order to be alive in this universe, we have to accept all of it. If we don't, then we're actually living in the world of the poor whale who is consigned to never getting out of its predicament, so all it has left is a rich fantasy life to distract it from its eventual demise. To me, that is a nightmare scenario. It's worth a lot of effort, every effort, to avoid getting stuck like that.

Freedom vs. Non-attachment

A lot of people equate freedom with non-attachment. There's a significant overlap there, but if you focus only on non-attachment, there's a tendency to go to that all-good side. We don't realize what our attachments are. Again this is a yoga problem. We have attachment and non-attachment together in us. Sometimes we are actually liberated by our mental scripting. We are freed up by some of the things that our mind has packaged very neatly and we have come to rely on. A classic example is tying our shoes. If you had to figure out how to do it every time, you would spend a lot of time relearning how to tie your shoes. But our very nice brain has got it all packaged and we can do it without even thinking. In a few seconds, it's done.

That's an attachment in a sense. Non-attachment, then, would mean that we have to look at these two strings sitting there on our shoe and have to very mindfully put one over the other and tuck it under and pull it tight. Well, okay, that can be called mindfulness. But why not revel in the fact that we don't have to worry about simple things like that? I remember when I was working simplistically on non-attachment, I shaved a different way every day trying to make sure I didn't get into any habits about shaving. Then I thought, well, doggone it, this is boring. I'll just shave the same way every day and get it over with quickly and move on to something more interesting.

In India there's a whole large caste of sannyasins who don't stay in any one place more than two or three days. Even during the monsoons, they keep wandering so that they don't become attached to anything. That's well and good, I suppose. A handful of them are probably very extraordinary people. But for most of us, that means that we wouldn't have any of the tools to really express ourselves. Because I have a home, I have equipment here I use for my best expression and it's the most satisfying thing I do. I'd be destitute without that and I wouldn't be contributing anything to anyone. So again, there's attachment and non-attachment. Both have their values. If you want to take non-attachment as a high value, it means don't be attached to the stupid things that keep you bound. It does not mean that you shouldn't be attached to anything.

There are people for whom complete non-attachment is fine, but there are many of us who use our attachments to give shape to our expression and accomplishment. Without an instrument for example, how can we make music? So the idea is to find what suits you best, not to take an abstract monolithic concept and follow it blindly. Bring in the nuances. Understand what's involved here and see all aspects of it. See how it best applies to you. The synthesis of dialectics—the synthesis of bringing opposites together—is to give us insights that we wouldn't have if we didn't stop to examine the situation. True yoga is an active mental process that also includes wonderful stretches of emptiness. But it's not all emptiness.

Just yesterday I was rereading Tom Robbins's first book, *Another Roadside Attraction*. In it, his science character, Marx Marvelous, says, "I craved the ultimate scientific luxury of being simultaneously involved and detached." I think that's a fantastic statement. Of course, it's a dialectic: involvement and detachment at the same time. It reminds me that great scientists are in many ways our true yogis. A lot of metaphysicians are living fantasy

LIBERATING OURSELVES

lives with make-believe behaviors that are kind of ridiculous. But the best scientists (and of course there are plenty of them living in fantasy worlds too!) are so interested in something that they're totally attached to it, pursuing it, learning about it and doing all of the work, while at the same time, they're intelligently restraining of their opinions and prejudices. That's is the detachment part.

By balancing attachment and detachment, they become even more excited and come to see more of the possibilities of whatever it is they're studying. So science really is very similar to the yoga philosophy. It's a shame that there's such a schism between science and yoga because it is so much the same work. I can see how many scientists and I are on the same path. We're all trying to understand what's going on in this baffling, amazing, complex soup that we live in. We both immerse ourselves in it and try not to get too wet.

5

The Role of The Chakras

Chakras are energy centers in the body. A lot of skeptics say there's no such thing as chakras. And that may or may not be the case. But this isn't based on believing or not believing in any particular thing. These ideas are metaphorical. They were devised by people who didn't have microscopes and telescopes and double-blind experimental procedures. Like all good scientists, those people were wise observers of things. They developed coherent and useful systems to explain what they observed.

The chakras are actually the centers of neural activity. My guru Nitya's talk on chakras includes the toes. Feet are famous for being wonderful areas of nerve endings: if they get rubbed, you feel good all over. But the first chakra is actually near the bottom tip of the spine, at the anus. The genitals, the area of the second chakra, are also famous as areas of sensual stimulation. The solar plexus, the third chakra, consists of quite few nerve ganglia in the middle of our abdomen. Nowadays the intestines themselves are seen as intelligent, as having their own small brain and operating independently from the brain that we carry around in our head. We experience a great deal through our gut instincts, so to speak. The heart, the fourth chakra, also has its own brain that can operate independently. Mimi Guarneri, a cardiologist from Scripps in California, wrote a wonderful book, *The Heart Speaks*, in which she talks about the little brain in the heart and its importance. The fifth chakra, the throat, contains the voice box, which is a very important center of vibrational intelligence. Just think of it as the source of our speech to gauge its importance. And yes, we know that speech is cooked up in our brain, but it passes through the fifth chakra to jump out into the environment. It's a point of contact with the world.

The sixth and seventh chakras are aspects of the brain. The sixth chakra is very close to the frontal cortex, centered between the eyebrows. No one had ever heard of the cortex 3,000 years ago, but it turns out to be where our conscious awareness is primarily located. And the ego that we're going to be talking about, with its conscious decision making, lies close to the forehead. So the guys who developed the system of chakras were pretty sharp to observe how and where the mind operates, without any fancy equipment.

Whether or not we think in terms of chakras, we do energize our bodies and we also inhibit that energy. We don't often think of what happens if we block or inhibit those areas of energy, but much of the illness and discomfort that we feel is due to the fact that we have inhibited our natural energies in a number of ways without even being aware of it. I'll highlight some of those inhibitions as we take a look at the chakras.

THE ROLE OF THE CHAKRAS

Chakra Meditation

There's a wonderful meditation that's quite easy to do, and it energizes the chakras intelligently. It involves taking each chakra and its element in sequence. The element of the first chakra, for example, is earth and the solid world. So we start at our body's first chakra and in our minds we move centrifugally out through the entire cosmos, finding the corresponding examples of that element all the way through the entire universe, and then centripetally bring it back to that spot, after which we move up to the next chakra.

With the first chakra it's solidity—solid elements—so as we sit there we can feel the chair or the ground we're sitting on, and with eyes closed and imagination engaged, we sweep out into a widening circle to take in the room we're in, the solid parts of it, the wood, the glass, and then we move out to the ground and throughout the entire world, the mountains and deserts and all of the land. And then we head farther out into the solar system, where all of the planets are solid bodies. We're quite sure there are planets around other stars. We let our minds expand out through the entire galaxy, and if we're capable, even into the multiverse. Then we bring our attention back from that far extension of our imagination in a swirling, centripetal movement back into our center.

We can do that with each chakra, and it will be different every time, as you always bring in new aspects of the element that corresponds to each. Doing this exercise has a remarkable impact on your chakras without any mystical folderol. I'll talk a little about each chakra, and include some of the symptoms of blocked energies in these places.

First Chakra: Root

The first chakra at the base of the spine, the *muladhara*, is your grounding place, your seat. In fact, the word *asana* means seat. It's where you sit down. That's your solid basis. And if you don't have a solid basis in your life, there's no sense of belonging. This not belonging, this displacement, is something that we see quite a bit nowadays. It's a kind of a psychic homelessness. No one feels like they belong anywhere, so they're wandering around searching for where that might be. That's an inhibition of the first chakra. By energizing that first chakra, we're not just putting hypothetic energy into it and making it pulsate; we're trying to connect with something that grounds us and let's us feel that we belong.

One of the big problems we have is that we are convinced that we belong somewhere other than where we are. This is a real area of practice, this coming back into ourselves. We actually belong right where we sit, right where our center is located. That is us. That is our essence, our ground. But we have forgotten it, and we're constantly looking elsewhere. We'll never find that by looking outward. So re-energizing the first chakra means finding where we belong, within our self. There's where our strengths are, where our spiritual comfort zone is. (Not our ego's comfort zone, which is a different thing. I think the ego is what diverts us from being centered in our chakras.) So again, this chakra business is not just a hypothetical or a spiritual or airy-fairy idea, but it has very practical implications. Chakras are essential to our well being psychologically as well as physically.

Second Chakra: Generative Organs

The second chakra is near the genitals. It's called the *svadhisthana*, which is the basis of our personality. When that area is unexpressed or inhibited, people develop sexual perversions because unconsciously they try to energize that area from the outside in, rather than from the inside out. Some of the more subtle evolutes of that kind of sexual domination or perversion are vengeance, cruelty, guilt and the urge to dominate and control. These are the unpleasant aspects of a blocked second chakra.

A blocked second chakra prevents us from having loving relationships with everything. Much of the viciousness exemplified by our species is the result of repressed sexuality. Repressed sexuality is repressed second chakra. Curing it is not just a matter of finding a healthy outlet for your sex, which is wonderful thing. I won't downplay that, but it's more about finding harmony with everything around you.

If you meditate on the second chakra as the water of life, you can trace that out in a centrifugal pattern starting with the water in you and the moisture in the air and the waters in your environment. Then expand it to the rivers, lakes and oceans of our world, and finally to other planets and galaxies. Think of water as a permeating layer of the universe, possibly even the life layer—the part that is alive and confers life (which is also what our genitals do). Now, bring your attention back from a galactic perspective to yourself, but always remember the principle of the universe that is bound to create life with its upsurging energy of delight. Harmonize it. And know that when you see yourself having negative reactions to different people, for example, you can trace them back to this center being blocked. Instead of thinking "That person is really horrible," go down to the source of your feelings and replace them or re-energize them with the loving sense of care and concern and joy for the life that you experienced in your meditation.

The Third Chakra: Solar Plexus

The third chakra, *manipura*, is the digestive fire, near the solar plexus. It's related to nourishment. Many of us are physically pretty well nourished. We are not, however, intellectually and spiritually so well nourished. Most of our interests (the interests our culture has invited us to enjoy) are quite superficial compared to our capacity for deep and transformative interests. Human beings have an amazing, astonishing ability to understand so many things and work with them and create new variations. Yet how often do we channel that ability into trivial pursuits? We pursue these trivialities and don't even realize that we are not being nourished. We might as well be eating cardboard. It fills us up and might even be made to taste good, but it really doesn't do anything for us.

So spiritually we're hungry all the time. Or else we have this really bloated feeling from lousy nourishment. But real nourishment is something we need to infuse in our lives and our selves. There are people who love knowledge and immerse themselves in their search understanding. Some are brilliant. They create amazing art and wonderful insightful articles and books and so on. What is it that you can study or do or feel or listen to? What is your nourishment? This is a very important spiritual determination. What am I nourished by? And can this thing that nourishes me also nourish others?

You can follow the element of fire from your solar plexus outwards through the world in the same way we did with rootedness and fluidity. Fire is the vibrational energy of matter. Reach out to the sources of warmth around you, going out to the sun. We see this energy all through our galaxy. Stars, for example, are points of fire—radiating and making it all happen. Feel that vibrational energy. Feel the wonder of the stars and bring it back into your self. You will feel nourished by that. And the more you are nourished, the more that nourishment radiates out from you and nourishes those around you. It's a really essential meditation.

Consider how different this feeling is from the responses we have to myriad stimuli and bits of information that we worship in our culture. We're so overwhelmed by spiritual junk food that we forget what it feels like to be really nourished. Let the discriminating fires of the intelligence in the third chakra lead you to distinguish what's worthwhile and what's not worthwhile.

The Fourth Chakra: Heart

The fourth chakra is the *anahata*. It is near the heart, and is associated with air and the sense of touch. When we're touched spiritually, we feel it in our heart. We consider the heart the seat of loving feelings. This region is also the passage for air—where air comes into the body and leaves it. Let's follow that air from our body out into the thin layer that surrounds our planet and makes life possible. The air surrounding the earth becomes thinner and thinner, but never quite disappears. I think the latest estimate is that "empty" space still has about six atoms per cubic meter. So there's still a little something floating around even in empty space. But air is concentrated around planets. Lucky, happy planets like ours are places where you can bring air into your body and come alive. And being alive is the essential thing!

So the heart is not just the seat of love; it's the seat of life and the vital energies that pass into and out of us. But, like the other chakras, it can be blocked. Most of us have experienced various degrees of blockage of our fourth chakra at different times in our life. And maybe often. Unrequited love is famous. In unrequited love, we have no outlet for our caring, and our thwarted passions tend to transform into defensive postures. We really want to love, but we're rejected, so we put up a barrier so that we're not hurt any further by the rejection of our caring nature.

I think a lot of this happens so early in our life that we have forgotten it. Small children are very loving. And it's often thwarted and rejected. So we learn to adopt postures of "How do I hold this back?" We actually spend a lot of energy restraining our natural impulse to love and embrace and care. We live in a world where the expression is often frowned on or barely tolerated. To some degree, it's repressed in everyone in the social arena.

So this is a wonderful place to meditate on how we have erected the barricades that we're stuck inside of and how we can dare to open those up in order to have a healthy fourth chakra and a healthy, caring attitude towards the planet without transgressing anyone else's fear of being contacted or cared for. It's actually something that bears a lot of consideration. We tend to be informed by and act according to our reactions. We have to learn to moderate them around others.

Sit down and intelligently meditate on this part of your life and see how, without being outwardly demonstrative, you can be inwardly loving and caring. That's a tricky balance to strike. But the upside is fantastic if you can accomplish it. And actually the cost of not doing it is very painful, so find the place of love and caring that is inside you and let it flourish.

LIBERATING OURSELVES

The Fifth Chakra: Throat

The fifth chakra, the *visuddhi*, is in the throat, the voice box. Communication is the essence of this chakra. The vibrations of words can be traced out from their origin. You can have a wonderful meditation on the sounds you hear in a room, thinking of the different vibrations of all the sounds of the world. It's so filled with sounds—we're in a very noisy part of our evolution—and you can travel all over with attention to the sound vibrations of this or that spot.

There are vibrations all through the universe even in places where there is no air to propagate sound. The sounds we can hear are located in planets with atmospheres, but everything is vibrating out there in space. The whole universe is vibrating. So your meditation can expand to the farthest horizon of the universe and then bring all of that tremendous energy back centripetally into your throat chakra.

Speech and what we say is almost as inhibited as our loving, caring feelings. Obviously, if we all talked all the time, we would have chaos, so we have to naturally restrain ourselves and only talk at appropriate moments. This is something that many people do not learn very well. I've worked with people who never could stop talking. It's a freaky thing. It's as though they wanted to reassure themselves of their existence by producing words. And you could never come to the end of a conversation so you just had to walk away from them. Their feelings weren't hurt because that happened to them all the time. Hopefully, that's not your problem.

Our speech, normal speech, can be thwarted in a variety of ways especially when we are kids. We've all heard, "Children should be seen and not heard" or "Don't bother us now." We sometimes give a wrong answer in school and everybody laughs at us. Inhibitions come thick and fast in those instances. It leads us to suppress our natural urge to speak spontaneously or relate some insight that's just occurred to us. It's a shame to lose that connection.

When our throat chakra is not energized in a healthy way, we feel that we're being ignored. We feel we're being ignored because we're not important.

We start to believe we're valueless, and in order to make that true, we suppress ourselves even more to prove that we really are worthless. We evolve a baseline attitude that "I'm not important, I don't belong, and I don't matter." We feel this is undoubtedly true as far as the outer world is concerned, but we also take on this attitude ourselves. We wind up with a divided consciousness, and we end up suppressing our own being for other people's benefit. We don't realize that by doing this, we're doing ourselves tremendous damage.

The meditation to restore a healthy throat chakra is to find value, meaning, and importance in our existence despite the fact that in many cases it's not welcomed by those around us. I think great teachers have found that balance. Of course, most of us are not in the position they are of being able to speak at length and having people in listen in rapture to what they say. But instead

LIBERATING OURSELVES

of beating up on ourselves or inhibiting ourselves because we are not great orators, let's acknowledge the true and legitimate regret we feel over not being able to express ourselves. And let's overcome it. Chanting is a very useful form of meditation to heal this blockage. Also singing, which is a modern form of chanting. Somehow energizing the throat chakra in a real way is very stimulating and helps us to feel whole again. The throat chakra is a very important center, and its healing is very important work.

The Sixth Chakra: Third Eye

The *ajna* is the third eye between the eyebrows. The sixth chakra is the fount of our wisdom. It is where our insight comes from. We have sight from our two eyes and we have insight in our third eye. This is not a culturally popular interpretation, but is a very useful one for those of use who are working to find liberation. We are fortunate to be able to undertake this work. It's a wonderful meditation to think of the brilliance of wisdom traveling from your third eye and swirling around through all the people nearby and all of the books, and computers that link you to all the other people on the planet and their intelligences and the places around the globe where these brilliant people are doing amazing things with their minds. You can project the fount of insight and wisdom out into the universe as a possible collective unconscious or universal mind that conceived this universe, and then recollect yourself filled with universal wisdom and insight.

THE ROLE OF THE CHAKRAS

The ancient Indians definitely thought consciousness was the primary condition of the universe and that it did not grow up from little particles put together in increasingly complicated ways. That it was the reverse of this process. Find your way into this concept any way you can. Some people might think of God at this point—this global awareness, this titanic, all-encompassing vision that is our universe—Without it, there is no universe. Now bring all that energy back into your sixth chakra.

The obvious outcome of an inhibited third eye is intolerance—especially religious intolerance. Because you are not in touch with your own wisdom, you feel like other people aren't either, whether or not they are, and that they shouldn't have a right to what they think. Because you don't have any personal experience, you're unsure. Because you've lost the connection with your own innate intelligence, you doubt everyone's ability to do that. High levels of doubt and cynicism toward everything are practically ubiquitous in our culture. That's the posture people adopt when they've lost contact with their own inner wisdom. They cannot accept that other people might be in tune with their wisdom. Therefore, everyone is a fool.

Interestingly, religious zealots are actually being energized by their secret doubts. They don't really believe what they're talking about or they would be much calmer and more tolerant of everyone else. There's an inverse relationship between your confidence and how aggressive you are. Oddly, when you're full of doubt, you try to activate your wisdom or your connection with what you're visualizing with a sort of violent clinging to those ideas. The cure is not to throw people's doubts back on them and make them worse, because they just become more aggressive, but to demonstrate the kind of inner connectedness in our lives that they could then participate in. I have found this to be a successful strategy. I grew up in a tough world where we thought that we should rub a person's nose in their mistakes and that that would help them. Of course, it did the opposite. If you actually look for the connection between you and the other person, it often bypasses a lot of the differences between you. You find a level of connection that is healing. At least at that moment, you can have contact with someone who you might otherwise think of as an enemy. That has the potential for far-reaching benefits.

We have to realize that everyone is just pretending. And it's really sad if you block any ingress that might help you heal that problem. The very people who are able to offer some amelioration of that condition are frequently ridiculed and turned away from. The ego is really talented at avoiding anything that threatens its adopted postures. A blocked sixth chakra is where that ego is most negatively energized to guide us away from what we really need.

What we crave deep down is to be in tune with our own intelligence and our own understanding and to know what's going on. And yet because of all the poses we've taken and all of the nets holding our "inner whale" hostage, we have learned to avoid what's most helpful to us. But there is hope in this work. Liberation is always possible.

The Seventh Chakra: Crown

Let's move on to the *sahasrara*, the thousand-petaled lotus of light at the top of the head. It is the aperture by which spiritual energies come and go in us. The seventh chakra is associated with transcendence because if you can sneak out through that aperture you can get out of your body. I had that experience once when I had taken some mescaline and was sitting in this stone tower up in the northwest corner of Connecticut. I was a young guy. I had heard about meditation, and I thought, "I've got to try this. I'm going to sit here and try meditating." The minute I did that, I suddenly was about 200 feet in the air, looking down at my body sitting on top of this stone tower. I'm afraid of heights and I had no preparation for this inner experience, so I freaked out! I thought "Oh, my god!" And I got back into my body as fast I could! I just zoomed back down and was mightily relieved to be back ion the ground. Had I been prepared, though, I might have gone on quite a journey!

If the seventh chakra is blocked—which it is in almost all of us because we have a nice, thick skull—we will not believe in transcendence. That inevitably leads to an acceptance of mediocrity. We become reconciled to our fate as just ordinary, ho-hum, not very exciting people in bodies who are walking around in a society trying to get our needs met and trying to have a little fun before we expire. But if you are willing to investigate the seventh chakra, you will see that we are mere shadows of what we could be and that life is potentially energized by vast infusions of light and love and ecstasy and bliss. That is our possibility. That is our destiny.

Unfortunately, many of us feel that this is not possible for us. This is a severely limiting attitude. We need to have some intimation that the sky is the limit and we are vast, amazing beings. We can free the whale. Even as I speak about this, the top of my head is tingling merrily.

The Chakras and Kundalini

The meditation of ancient India in which you chant the Gayathri mantra at each chakra while focusing on it is a good way to begin to tune into the chakras. Energizing the chakras and looking for the types of inhibitions that block them enables us to move through some or all of those inhibitions in an acceptable, safe format that is uplifting and wonderful. It's well worth sitting down occasionally (or often!) and spending a little time in meditation. You can listen to a Gayathri meditation guided by my guru here: https://sites.google.com/site/gurusclass/music. There are some other links on my website: scottteitsworth.tripod.com/id2.html.

The chakras, which are all located more or less along the spine, are linked together by an energy that's referred to as kundalini

THE ROLE OF THE CHAKRAS

energy. The Indians feel that we start our life with our first breath, and that first breath includes an in-rushing of kundalini through the seventh chakra at the top of the head. It pours down through the spine and coils up like a snake in the *muladhara* at the base of the spine. The theory is that as we grow, this kundalini energy comes out of its tight knot and gradually travels up the spine to activate the different chakras, and this is responsible for our development.

The first chakra is pretty much concerned with the basics of existence, so our first interests center on survival. The second chakra involves the beginning of personality—what we like and don't like—which lays the groundwork for our ego. Then the third chakra becomes energized: the intelligence, our intellectual side, our understanding. We begin to make sense of our world. The fourth, the heart, chakra is when we begin to have concerns for someone other than ourselves. We start to include others in our self-definition. This expansion, this learning to care for others in the family, the community and the world, is the fourth chakra coming awake. The fifth chakra is the site of meaning. We begin to want to understand life and the world. And ultimately when the highest parts of the spine at the sixth chakra are stimulated, we begin to get real insight.

If the kundalini rises to the seventh chakra, it can escape out of the body (as it did on my youthful adventure). A lot of kundalini meditation is designed to encourage this energy to course up and down the spine. You visualize it and encourage it to come out and travel up and down as a way of energizing your chakras. But be careful. This is an exceedingly intense energy if it released, and it is something that most people are not prepared to handle.

This is why I recommend energizing your chakras through the kind of intelligent meditation to heal the psyche that I described earlier, rather than something mechanical that will send a bolt of energy to rise through the spine and "light everything up." There's a cautionary book written by Gopi Krishna called *Kundalini: The Evolutionary Energy in Man*, about the dangers of explosive kundalini activation. His kundalini was switched on in a radical way and it almost ruined his life. It was like he was on fire all the time, though he did eventually get it under control. Don't let this happen to you! Instead, let the movement of the kundalini energy increase naturally, in small quantities, as your inner guidance system permits. We are brilliantly designed to evolve and make use of our energies in so many ways that are wonderful. And just by doing that, your inner guidance system measures out exactly the amount of energy that you need. Not too much, not too little. So if I were going to do kundalini yoga, I would certainly be very cautious and think of it as very small quanta, little packets of energy, not the entire snake. A snake is the small form of a dragon. It's really a dragon in there. And unless you want to ride a dragon, be very careful.

6

Healing the Ego

The Role of the Intellect

Like the whale caught in the fishing nets, by adolescence our functioning is very much constrained. The point of any yoga exercise is to find ways to free ourselves from the nets that entrap us and the burdens that weigh us down. There's a simple approach in Vedanta that I think is quite helpful. In it, we visualize our system as consisting of all its parts. These parts are really all one thing, but they do represent different aspects of who we are. We have a body. We have senses connected to the surface of that body that are neurologically connected to a center of operations that we recognize now as the brain. We consider the brain to be the center of consciousness and the center of what we think of as the ego. The ego is the sense of I, or the sense of self. It's the local feeling of who we are. The mind is sometimes the tool of the ego. The mind is the coordinator of the senses in Indian theory. It's not the whole brain. It's the very amazing part that interprets all of the vibrations coming through the nerves into the brain and fashions a plausible image of the world for us to interact with.

LIBERATING OURSELVES

The ego then is a kind of center of the system—certainly from our own perspective it is. The intellect in this system is actually the bridge into the depths of our consciousness. The presumption is that at the core or center of our being is a connection with the totality, a state of oneness with everything. We call it 'the Absolute' for want of a better term, because words like God or Truth may imply non-God and non-Truth aspects. 'God' is especially well known as a problematic term for many people. So 'The Absolute' is a very neutral term for whatever the source of our being is in the center of us.

The intellect, then, is the part of us that directs our attention, not toward the surface of the body and its interaction with the world, but toward the center of ourselves, ideally opening up our blockages to allow inspiration and guidance from that region into our lives. Here's where the ego, in our Western model, becomes a problem. In the West, the assumption is that the intellect is a kind of rational tool of the ego instead of a gateway to higher powers within our brains and bodies. Granted, scientific perceptions of the intellectual aspect of the brain are changing. Science is coming to understand that there are very powerful things going on in the brain, energies that run most of our lives without our volition, our ego, being involved at all. But psychotherapy still uses the model that the intellect is better "turned off" to allow for the relaxation of blockages. Unfortunately, since the intellect is the part of us that bridges our conscious self to our core reality, turning off the intellect blocks the connecting link to our full self.

In the Indian system, a healthy ego is aware of its limitations, as well as its value. In the Indian practice and through meditation the ego is brought into the right relation with the other parts of the brain, and a balance is established. There is a serious problem when the ego is perceived as the block between us and God (our deeper reality), and leaders seek to dissolve it. That's actually a horrifying idea. You've probably all seen zombie movies. Zombies have no ego. This effort to eradicate ego leads to tragedies like the cult phenomenon.

The Role of the Ego

I like to think of the ego's role as the switchboard or the clearinghouse where input from the body and from the intellect is pouring in and we're working to optimize what we do with it. The ego needs to be healthy. It needs to be honored. But it certainly does not need to be any bigger than it should be. When you look at the history of its development, when we pop out of the womb, we're pretty much undeveloped in that regard. The initial development of the ego is based on pure selfishness, self-interest. We don't have complex reasoning going on or much familiarity with our world. So we start out as purely selfish beings. Our main interest is to attain pleasurable states and avoid painful states. In fact, for the early ego, that becomes the whole game: achieving pleasure and rejecting pain. It's all about attraction and repulsion. We become masters at getting what we want and avoiding what we don't want. Unfortunately, that is based on limited information and the often painful circumstances that children are subjected to. This prompts us to develop distorted ego-based notions of what we should do and how we should live.

Our egos have become a protective shield directing us away from anything that promises to be problematic and toward something that will give us a fast reward. In spiritual development, we are looking at a longer learning curve. We have to somehow relinquish that fascination with instant gratification and the rejection of painful undertakings. People who climb mountains or do other strenuous exercises like running marathons are familiar with that in a somatic sense: you do something that is strenuous and difficult and not much fun for a while, but eventually you get to this wonderful place that makes it all worthwhile. The *Bhagavad Gita* says that's the sattvic, the best, type of happiness. It comes from dedicated work—from paying our dues and achieving something meaningful.

Today, in our Western culture, we have so many toys to play with, so many stimulations, so many clever new things to attract our attention, that the world is becoming more and more superficial. Even spiritual practices are superficial. They're based on clichés and sound bites and repetitive practices—things which are fairly simple and don't actually touch us down deep. This is all because the ego is actually running the show. And the ego, being us, knows exactly how to steer us in any direction it wants without our being aware that it's doing it. Here's where some outside influence, a teacher or a guide, is really essential. The whale isn't able to take its own nets off; somebody has to help it with that. We humans can take off the nets, but somebody has to help us recognize that they're there.

The Work We Can Do with the Ego

First, we must recognize the ego's limited focus and see how it has basically built us into a box where we're afraid of things that don't fit our model. Then we have to befriend our true selves as who we really are, instead of the false persona that the ego has constructed for us. This is perhaps the most critical stage of our development. We tend to agree with society that we should hate our bad parts and love our good parts. But in spiritual life, we have to love all of ourselves as we are—which consists of good and bad all mixed together. Once you start looking at how you needlessly reject yourself, you will be shocked by how deep the rejection goes. We've learned to ward off a lot of criticism by criticizing ourselves before somebody else gets the opportunity. So that whole wall of false of attitudes needs to be worked off to begin to have a healthy ego.

Accept yourself as you are. Once that is in place, recognize a core within you that maintains a boundary of acceptability. It's initially not very large, but it may include your family and friends and possibly your community. You can extend this boundary to include more things and more of the world around you. Do it intelligently. You're not just moving a fence farther and farther out. You're beginning to think, "Okay, the reason I'm afraid of these people is because my ego tells me that they're different from me or their behavior shocks me, but I see that they're doing what they're doing because of certain factors in their lives. They're as helpless as anyone else to affect the situations they are caught in. Both they and I would love to come to a perfect Garden of Eden state of mind, but somehow we've been diverted far from it and don't know how to get back to it." As you begin to feel this about other people, especially those outside your boundary of acceptability, your compassion grows, your ability to include them in your sense of who you are grows.

The enlargement of the ego in this way is a very healthy thing. This is not a selfish enlargement of your importance over everything else. It's putting everything on an equal footing. We start out with our egos feeling sure that we are the only thing that matters. But when we extend that importance, that validity, to everyone and every thing around us, fear is lessened, resistance dissolves, and the nets begin to fall away. (A cautionary note here… I'm not talking about throwing your fences open to all the weird things in this world. There are, in fact, many real physical and psychic dangers. Let your intellect guide you. Seek help. Find a source of valid wisdom. Be informed by that core of acceptability within you.)

Fear of Ego Dissolution

The ego fears dissolution. It fears its loss more than anything else. So if we have a program that professes to do away with the ego, the ego is not going to accept it. When the ego is under threat and feels persecuted, it twists the truth, and it produces all the responses that we see in nations at war: false flag operations, black ops and sabotage, viciousness.... It all comes out when the ego feels threatened. It's interesting that nations are like gigantic egos. There are so many parallels between the selfish, mean-spirited acts of the individual ego and the acts of nations. I think that's why the Taoists feel that by changing yourself, you change your world. There really is some parallel there. So do away with all of the attacks on the ego. Learn to accept your own ego, even though everyone around you is still playing the same game of let's pretend we're not who we actually are. It takes courage to relax our defense system. But if we don't, we are doomed to a mediocre life and a life of conflict.

Detachment

This leads me to the notion of detachment. There's much to commend detachment, but it's a little tricky to get it right. The ego's simplistic version of detachment is to shut out the world and our relationship to it. This leads to some real spiritual dead ends. Detachment should never be based on blocking things out. The true detachment comes from finding our passion: something that really activates our interest and the joy of being attuned with the core of truth in us. Whenever that happens, our focus goes to that core, and irrelevancies—distractions to which we would otherwise attach our attentions—just vanish, like mist before the sun. Detachment, then, should be a natural secondary effect of absorption and not something we strive to implement for its own sake.

Neurologically, that's how we rewire out brains. Not by trying to *not* do something. When you do that you're putting energy into the same neurons that had developed to enable that behavior, so you're actually reinforcing what you want to do away with. True detachment means moving toward what you want to bring into your life. When you do that, those old neurological pathways wither away and eventually are replaced by other types of abilities. The ancient vision was totally in line with the modern understanding of the brain,. The *Bhagavad Gita* teaches, "Don't just shut things down. Don't resist. Look for the One beyond, and the One beyond is within the center of your being. When you're in tune with that, when you're doing the creative acts and living the way you know is right, then all the other extraneous, things fall into place naturally—without conflict and without any extra effort."

I've been in some spiritual communities where it was widely insisted that if you noticed a problem, you were creating the problem. You caused the problem just by being aware of it. But you can't ignore challenges and hope they don't exist. That's just a way of turning your back on people and situations that may really need your attention and care. It's an ego posture. Our spiritual natures cares very, very much. Now, this doesn't mean you have to obsess about every problem in the world either. But we do have to strike a balance of understanding: there are problems that we should be doing our best to ameliorate while we retain our sense of who we are and our good feelings about life.

After all, this is it. This is our life. It's supposed to be wonderful. We should be making it wonderful. But for most of us at least, making it wonderful based on turning our backs on people is not a successful strategy. You want to be open and caring, and at the same time, not despairing. It's completely possible and perfectly reasonable. The brain is already an inhibitory mechanism. Aldous Huxley was right. A well-ordered brain is an excellent "reducing valve," taking a vast amount of input, producing a simple readout of the most essential parts of everything that's coming in to us, and presenting that to our conscious mind. We should welcome what it shows us, rather than trying to close ourselves off from it.

Reverse Inhibition

It's important to understand that I'm not talking about inhibiting thoughts and responses. Inhibiting is actually the opposite of what we need to do. We are already severely inhibited. We need to inhibit the inhibiting part. So it's a reversal of inhibitions. As I mentioned earlier, a study was done in which the researchers used MRIs to study the brain activity of people taking psychedelics. The researchers anticipated seeing many parts of the brain lighting up because of all the visions and exciting things that go on during a psychedelic experience. To their amazement, there was actually much less activity in the brain because the psychedelics were actually quieting the normal pattern of inhibitions. When inhibitions are put to rest, the natural high energy that we are constructed from comes back into our consciousness. It's always been there. We've just learned to screen it out and suppress it in order to get through ordinary life. Meditation is also a way to quiet that part of us (the inhibitory part) that's blocking the amazingly intelligent energy we are made of.

So detachment actually should be "turning on" in a way. It's a way to open us up to more and more to the miracle of existence. We are not obsessing about trivia because we are focused on the spectacular beauty of life—beauty that we embody and are meant to express. We really are expressions of the divine. It's up to us to find ways to make that into a great light show for the benefit of ourselves as well as the world around us.

Making Good Decisions

The entire eighteen chapters of the *Bhagavad Gita* is an instructional guide to teach the disciple Arjuna how to make good decisions. In the beginning, Arjuna doesn't know what to do. And Krishna, his guru, says, "Of course you don't. Let me tell you what's going on here and then you will be able to make good choices." Arjuna says, "Sign me up. I really need this." So they go through a lot of amazing explorations and the result is a gorgeous presentation of the philosophy I've been pointing to in this lecture. At the very end, Krishna says, "Okay, you're ready to go. You are now wise enough to make your own decisions. So what do you think?" And Arjuna says, "Oh man, this is great. I really feel like I understand now. So what do you want me to do?"

Krishna looks at him in amazement. "Are you not paying attention? I'm not here to tell you what to do. *You* have to tell you what to do. *You* have to make decisions that are worthwhile. *You're* the one who decides. *You* look at everything closely, *you* critically scrutinize it, *you* come to understand the situation, then *you* decide." That decision, I should add, comes from the depths. *Your* depths. The decision is not just between A, B, C or D on some kind of SAT test. Your whole being is brought into making decisions in important matters. Of course, if you're at the store deciding between two different soups, that's a different thing. But in terms of the great arc of your life, that's what it is. You've been trained to follow orders and to do what other people want you to do. Now, not suddenly, but after careful introspection and involvement of all the parts of yourself, you have the opportunity, as a wise adult, to learn how to make your own decisions, to set your own course.

This actually brings about a radical change in your life. It's what we call spiritual. It feels so great when you can make your own decision or when you actually just go with your own inner promptings and you know—really *know*—that they're good ones; not just selfish new ones in disguise. This is the real deal. You've vetted them, and they're okay. And you can go with them. It's a great feeling. It's like coming back to yourself. It's like being

LIBERATING OURSELVES

yourself again. It's the feeling you had in the womb when you were untroubled by things. It's freedom from the nets. It's a great feeling. And it's also a challenge. New opportunities will find their way to you in a steady stream, and that's how you'll know you're on the right track.

Opting for Freedom

Most people don't know how to handle freedom. The Indian caste system as it was conceived was a scheme for assessing how much people could handle freedom. The *sudras,* the servile caste, was composed of people who didn't want to make their own decisions at any cost. They wanted somebody else to tell them what to do. The *vaisyas,* the merchant caste, was composed of people who enjoyed a measure of independence, but who needed to keep it within strict bounds. Some *kshatriyas,* who we would now think of as our politicians and sports and movie stars, were called warriors in the old days. They had a greater measure of freedom, but were still confined within a social context of operation. *Brahmins* were the religious types, who resembled the professors and judges and academics of our day. They had even more independence—independence of thought, for example. Finally the *sannyasins,* the renunciates, were those who insisted, "I'm going to live free and as I am prompted to do by my inner being. I'm not going to follow the rules in any sense. I have renounced all nets."

The degree to which people are unable to handle freedom is probably passed on via custom and a kind of passive education through generations. I actually think we all enter into life moving towards freedom, but that movement is usually suppressed. People learn that freedom is a painful or dangerous thing and they become so fearful of making bad decisions and being punished for them that they opt for what might be called a low caste attitude over the risks of freedom.

So there is a continuum of freedom from total enslavement to absolute liberty. Where do you find yourself on this scale of values? And where would you prefer to be? Most of us cannot handle perfect freedom, but we'd like some, and some of us would like a lot. Choosing how free we want to be is one of our most important decisions. Do you even know where you've decided to be on the freedom continuum? And do you even recognize the ways in which you have bartered away your freedom for comfort's sake?

7

Concluding Thoughts

Keeping a Light Touch

Questions like how to balance responsibility and freedom can bring you down. Don't let it. It is very important to keep a lighthearted, humorous attitude about all this work. The more you get depressed by the weight of the world, the more blockages you create, and the more you become closed off. Keep a "light touch" when dealing in spiritual matters. Be earnest in your commitment and laugh when you're stymied.

Humor opens things up. To move from dogged taskmastering to laughter is a beautiful process. There's an old saying that "a saint who is sad is a sad saint." Let's forgo the sad saints. My guru had an amazing sense of humor. He knew how to yuk it up and tell jokes. He smiled, actually beamed, a lot, and just looked happy, except when he was railing about the idiocies of his disciples. There is something to be said for feeling great, and if you're not, maybe there's something missing from your program. Yes, the world is full of tragedies and depressing, horrifying things, and we participate in some of those, but we can learn to view them either as oppression or opportunity.

If you have a lighthearted approach, even in difficult situations, you can avoid resentment. Again, you have to come to know yourself. You have to sense what's going to work and what isn't. I think that, in general, having a good sense of humor and feeling great go together. Yes, we see images of famous saints as withdrawn, otherworldly, detached, neutral beings, but they testify to asceticism—which was an important aspect of early Christianity and Hinduism. Their lives make impressive stories, as do the spectacular feats they supposedly performed. People like miracles. But, truly, I think that having a really good attitude is the best miracle of all.

I remember seeing an image of Jesus Christ laughing. He had a big smile on his face and a twinkle in his eye. I had never seen that. I had only seen sad, miserable images of this guy nailed to the cross. Well, he wasn't like that all the time. Nevertheless it shocked a lot of people to see a happy image of him. But why not? I think if you understand your place in this world, it's funny. I mean, we don't even exist and yet we certainly seem to exist. All these paradoxes could make you cry or they could make you laugh. We're caught in this miracle called the universe. Let it be amusing. Enjoy it.

Spirituality and Balance

People think spirituality is a lot of different things. I think spirituality is bringing ourselves back into balance when our struggles knock us out. A lot of people think they're supposed

LIBERATING OURSELVES

to always be in balance, and a few people maybe are. The rest of us are not. We get knocked off balance by many things. Anything unexpected or tragic will do it. But how fast we recover is the mark of our spirituality, not whether or not we're affected by it. This is really the crux of the matter when it comes to healthy versus artificial detachment. People think they're not supposed to react and that's not right. Of course we're supposed to react, but we're not supposed to stay in a reactive position forever. We're supposed to get back into balance. That's healthy detachment.

I had someone once ask me, "My mother is about to die. Is it okay for me to be upset about this?" Come on, man. Of course. Yes. Cry. Freak out. Tear your hair. Be upset. But just don't stay in that place. You are *supposed* to feel. That really brought it home to me. "Aren't we supposed to be perfectly angelic at all moments, even when our parents die?" No! It's okay to freak out. You should. In fact, if you're not upset, there's something really amiss there. You're closed off to one of the most dramatic moments of your life, detached precisely when you should be most engaged.

In order for us to break free from the types of mental constructs (like artificial detachment) that hold us back, we must be actively involved in our lives. The default setting, which is very popular in spiritual life, is stagnation. Our brains will not change unless we work to rewire them. That work has to be paired with the understanding that conscious intent actually suppresses our contact with our inner self. There has to be a fine balance between working and not working, trying and not trying. We won't get it right on the money the first or the hundred and first time, so we go back and forth, again and again. But we don't get stuck. We work at it. And we also have to understand that the limitations of our vision are actually putting up blocks over the inner truth that is trying to express itself so we can leap around in the ocean of life like a whale that's been freed.

I hope I've made it clear that I do not espouse any particular path. I'm not an evangelist for Narayana Guru, though I highly recommend his and Nataraja Guru's and Nitya Chaitanya Yati's philosophy. It's very helpful stuff. But there's no specific path. There's no one program. Everything we do and everything we learn is an integral part of our path. Buddhism and Vedanta are similar in many ways. In the West, Buddhism is now quite popular; Vedanta less so. The Buddhists are very well organized and they put things in clear, linear patterns in their teaching and writings. It's easily accessible to people who begin with book readings or practice, whereas Vedanta is much more fluid and seemingly haphazard. The disorganized approach has its advantages, because once you think you know what the program is, there's a tendency to go to sleep, in a sense. But it goes against our grain in the highly organized West.

Again, I'm not recommending Buddhism or Vedanta. The key to everything is to meet each opportunity with an open mind and a desire to optimize the outcome. Not to optimize what we get out of it, but to optimize our appreciation of it so that we will come to know what's needed and what we can contribute. We're raised to want to be on the winning team and to be affiliated with

LIBERATING OURSELVES

this or that or the other thing, but we are at our best as free and independent operators. We can take wisdom from all the many places where it resides. Ultimately, all paths lead us to understand that I am I in as much as I am also you and your neighborhood or country or world or universe. The fluid feelings and thoughts that move through our chakras are the very powers that create and nourish civilizations. And the nets that bind and paralyze us are the assumptions and interpretations that we absorb and recreate for ourselves in our own private selves, countries, worlds and universes.

So, have compassion for yourself as you would for the whale. Recognize its majesty and know that it is yours. Know that freedom from the nets is possible. Choose it. Allow it. And enjoy it. Permit yourself to laugh!

About the Author

SCOTT TEITSWORTH has been a lifelong student of Indian philosophy and modern science under the tutelage of Nitya Chaitanya Yati, a disciple of Nataraja Guru.

Obsessed from an early age with the mysterious connection uniting the realms of spirit and matter—more commonly framed as the unconscious and the conscious mind—Scott has spent a lifetime investigating their interrelationship. His search led him to the lineage of Narayana Guru, from South India, that expounds a revolutionary confection of modern science and ancient wisdom focused on real-life issues.

Scott lives in Portland, Oregon, where he and his wife, poet Deborah Buchanan, have taught classes on the cream of Indian wisdom since the 1970s. A retired firefighter EMT and a classical pianist, Scott has taught the entire *Bhagavad Gita* over several decades in Portland. He offers a radically different interpretation that treats the *Gita* as a work of science and psychology with an spectacularly progressive slant.

He has presented his work at the University of Illinois, and in India at CMS College.

Scott is the also the author of *Krishna in the Sky with Diamonds: The Bhagavad Gita as Psychedelic Guide*; *The Path to the Guru: The Science of Self-Realization According to the Bhagavad Gita*; and *Coming Back to Ourselves: Finding Authentic Direction in the Chaos of Being*.

For More Information

Scott Teitsworth

scottteitsworth.tripod.com

Wetware Media

www.wetwaremedia.com

www.ingramcontent.com/pod-product-compliance
Lightning Source LLC
Chambersburg PA
CBHW021131300426
44113CB00006B/377